Quick Tips
FOR GENEALOGISTS

EDITED BY JULIANA S. SMITH

ancestry publishing

Library of Congress Cataloging-in-Publication Data

Quick tips for genealogists / edited by Juliana S. Smith.
    p. cm.
Includes index.
  ISBN 10: 1-59331-155-9 (pbk. : alk. paper)
  ISBN 13: 978-1-59331-155-1
  1. Genealogy—Miscellanea. I. Smith, Juliana Szucs, 1962–
CS14.Q53 2003
929'.1'072—dc22

                                                  2003021599

Published by
Ancestry Publishing, a division of
The Generations Network, Inc.
360 West 4800 North
Provo, Utah 84604
www.ancestry.com

Second printing 2008
10 9 8 7 6 5 4 3

Printed in Canada.

Contents

Preface

When the "Ancestry Quick Tip" segment of the *Ancestry Daily News* began appearing back on 24 August 1999 it was an immediate success. I had originally anticipated that I would be supplying most of the tips, getting a few here and there from readers; since that first day, however, all of the tips that have run in the newsletter have come from readers. Not a day goes by that I don't get tips from around the world.

The Quick Tips have turned the newsletter into more than just another e-zine, but rather a community effort, with family historians helping each other. Occasionally we post a request for tips on a particular topic, and I'm invariably inundated with innovative solutions for the problems family historians share. The enormous response we regularly receive demonstrates the kind and giving nature of genealogists everywhere.

With topics that range from where to locate resources to search tips to preservation to computer safety, quick tips have covered nearly every aspect of family history. *Ancestry Daily News* readers have become a network of friends who share their expertise with all of us. We take their thoughts with us to the library, to the cemetery, to courthouses, as we travel to research in our ancestral hometowns, or as we research from the comfort of our homes in our pajamas in front of the computer.

When several readers wrote in to suggest that the tips would make a good book, the editorial staff at Ancestry set to work and you are now holding the result. I hope that this collection inspires you as it inspires me in my own research. I personally owe many of the contributors a debt as I continue to benefit from their experience in my own research. Thanks to all of you who have taken the time to share your thoughts with all of us!

—*Juliana Smith*
Editor, Ancestry Daily News

Wedding Date Engraved on Ring

I never knew when my mother's parents were married; the date seemed to be lost forever. Years ago, before I was interested in genealogy, my uncle (my mother's brother) gave me my grandparents' wedding rings. He had retrieved them both when his mother passed away. At the time, I put them into the safe deposit box for safekeeping.

Many years later, when my daughter was planning her wedding, I offered the rings to her and her fiancé to use. They were both thrilled to own these concrete symbols of our family genealogy. In the process of inspecting these rings, I noticed that there were two dates engraved on the inside of each ring. My mother explained that in "the old country" (Germany), you wore a simple gold band on the ring finger of your right hand as an indication of engagement, and when you married, the gold band was transferred to the ring finger of your left hand. So the two dates engraved on the inside of the two gold bands were the date of their engagement and the date of their marriage. Using the later date on the inside of the gold bands, I sent away to the proper authorities in the city where they were married, and received a copy of their wedding certificate. You never know where you will find genealogical data!!!

—*Barbara Algaze*
Los Angeles, California

Who Will Get the Family Heirloom?

Upon the death of my dear mother at ninety-nine-and-one-half years old, I inherited, among other things, her Springerle Rolling Pin. As I already had one that she had bought me earlier, I was trying to find a way to pass on the pin as an heirloom, as well as the tradition of making Springerle cookies at Christmas time, to one of my three sons. Since I didn't want to show favoritism, so here's what I did.

I put three recipe cards in three envelopes and let my sons choose one (they had no idea what they were choosing). One card had the Springerle Recipe on it, which made him the winner of the Springerle Rolling Pin and gave him the duty of making Springerle cookies each Christmas. With the rolling pin I gave the following letter on Christmas letterhead paper:

Springerle Cookies—Our Tradition
As a tradition, I should like to pass on Grandma Caroline (Lena) Mische-Kuhn's Springerle Rolling Pin. With this pin comes an obligation to make Springerle cookies each year at Christmas time, and give some to each of your peers. The first years I shall help the recipient of this Springerle Rolling Pin make the cookies, if they would like. (I have a very sturdy beater.) This Springerle Rolling Pin is to be an heirloom from Grandma Kuhn and passed on to a descendant of our family, with the same wish (and tradition) to make the cookies each Christmas, and eventually pass on the rolling pin to help a new recipient make the cookies. If you, or any recipient does not want to carry on this tradition they have the right to pass on this heirloom to some other member of our family. With love from Marilyn P. Kuhn-Senn. (My note on the bottom says to whom it went and the date).

—Marilyn Senn

Photos of Your Ancestor's Arrival Ship

A good resource for locating information on the ships of our ancestors is *Passenger Ships of the World*, published by the George H. Dean Company. The INS Immigration and Passenger List documented my dad's arrival on the Zeeland in 1905. The library of the Steamship Historical Society of America, Inc. lists two ships named Zeeland—1865 and 1901, with several dates when the two ships were renamed. After determining which ship was the correct vessel, I ordered a photo of the ship from: Steamship Historical Society Collection

University of Baltimore Library
1420 Maryland Ave
Baltimore, MD 21201-5779
410-837-4268
http://archives.ubalt.edu/steamship/collect.htm

Provide them with as much information as you have, i.e., name of the ship, date of sailing, ports of departure and arrival, etc. They will research and respond by advising you of their results and the costs for ordering photos. Their collection consists of more than 200,000 prints, slides, and negatives. When I placed my order, the fee was $16 for an 8x10, less for smaller sizes, and more for 11x14.

—*Sylvia Furshman Nusinov*

Preserve Home Memories in a Video

When we first moved into our present-day house, we took a "walking and talking" video to show to our friends and relatives who lived far away. I've also taken pictures during remodeling projects and kept samples of wallpaper, etc., to document changes. Every year now, I also take seasonal pictures outside, especially of my flowerbeds, using our digital camera. (This also helps me to plant for next year's flowerbeds.)

If you decide to create a "walking and talking" video for the home of a recently deceased relative, why not also take a few moments to check every nook and cranny for items that your relative may have hidden for safe keeping? Be sure to check inside things also: pockets of clothing, books, envelopes, cards, old notebooks. You may be surprised at what you find. When my parents died, we did this and found money, old pictures, and notes that had meaning for me as a genealogist.

—Carol Smiley

On Saving Art and School Work

I have two children, ages ten and seven. I realized long ago that it was impossible to save every piece of artwork or school project. I needed to find a way to acknowledge their hard work before I snuck them into the trash can.

At our house, we have designated one door for displaying their seasonal artwork or an A+ on the spelling test. This is the door by the kitchen that leads to the garage. We tape to it anything the kids are proud of and want to display. When there is no more room on the door, we snap a picture of it. The projects and pictures on the door come down and mysteriously disappear in the middle of the night, but we have a picture in the photo album so that we never forget. And the process starts all over again.

I have boxes for the best of the best. There is one box in each kids' closet. When I absolutely can't part with something that they have done, in the box it goes. When the box is full, I tape it up, label it and put it in the attic. Then, a new box goes in the closet. Some day, when I'm retired, I'll get those boxes down and look through them. I already look forward to it.

— *Teale Kocher*

Clues in Your Relatives' Old Books

Ask family members if they have old books. From the owners' inscriptions in old books I have learned: my mother's childhood street address in Detroit, a great-uncle's middle name, the name of my grandmother's grammar school, the town where my great-great-grandfather taught, and a distant relative's childhood nickname.

And what fun to find hints of personality for little-known relatives: notes to schoolmates, doodles of dragons and princesses, inspirational gift dedications and flowery signatures. My portable scanner lets me copy these on the spot.

Just as valuable are the relatives' recollections as they bring out the books. My mother recalled that during the Depression, her working mother used meager spending money to bring home "armloads of books" from failed bookstores, so that her children grew up steeped in tales of Greek gods and the Knights of the Round Table.

—*Janet Wright*

Sharing Birthday Memories

Just this week my daughter came home from out of state for a weekend visit, coinciding with her twentieth birthday. I wanted to do something special, different, and unique to make it memorable. I asked each person we had invited to dinner to write a bit about a personal birthday memory of my daughter. It could be funny, sad, short, or long. After dinner, she opened each card or note and read that person's birthday memory out loud to everyone there. They all loved it! There was much laughter, tears, and conversation the entire evening.

After the notes were all read, everyone started saying, "I remember one time when …" Afterward, my daughter thanked me for such a great evening with family, and we rehashed the stories that had been told. Since the initial memories were written on note cards, I immediately scanned them to include in my family history and wrote out those others that were just talked about in our conversations. It was the best evening of conversation, and we all learned something about other family members. Try it and see if you don't get similar results.

—*Kristine Johnson-Burrill*

Lists Document Domestic Travelers

As passenger arrival lists for various ports become available, we tend to think of them only as a tool for finding immigrant ancestors, but they can document domestic travelers, too. Our family legend said that my great-great-grandfather was born in New York and went west to work on the boats on the Mississippi. I had assumed a cross-country trip. But on a hunch I checked a database of a ship's passenger arrivals in New Orleans and found him there in 1838, at age twenty-one, arriving in New Orleans by sea. (This entry also confirmed the year of his birth.) Ships were a handy means of travel between ports, not just across the ocean.

—Toby Webb

Locating Institutionalized Ancestors

Another researcher and I have teamed up to find my husband's great-grandmother Lydia on as many census records as possible. The biggest problem we came across was that she was in a mental hospital at one point of her life. How do you search for someone in a mental hospital on a census? Tenacity.

Older members of the family told us that Lydia's youngest daughter was living with an older sister when Lydia was hospitalized. Apparently this information was noted on the 1920 census. Little Ollie Tiffee was ten and living with older sister Rosa Ragle. So it was the 1920 census we wanted to search. Luckily, it is indexed. But, unluckily for us, Lydia wasn't in the index anywhere.

My research buddy found a site about historical asylums: <www.historicasylums.com/>. And in searching Oklahoma, we found three: Central State Hospital, Norman; Eastern State Hospital, Vinita; and Western State Psychiatric Center, Fort Supply.

Since the family was in the eastern part of Oklahoma on other census records, we searched the eastern site and found Lydia. The men and women were divided on the census pages and then listed alphabetically. I don't know why, but not all the patients were in the index. The census showed that she was married, but we know she was widowed by then, as her husband, Joseph Tiffee, died in 1914. The census says she could not read or write, yet I have some "home remedies" in her handwriting. This information makes you wonder if while she was institutionalized, she was unable to read or write.

—*Linda Garrett*

View the Original Source

I was lucky enough to be able to travel this summer to some of the places where my ancestors lived in South Dakota. I had already looked at cemetery indexes online and found some tombstones of my ancestors and assumed that what was listed, i.e., birth and death dates, was all the information available. Imagine my surprise when I located my Catherine (Hartmann) Bergold's tombstone and listed on her tombstone was "Born in Swineforth Germany." I had never seen a birthplace listed on a headstone before and haven't since.

My message is to check in person, even if you think you know what is on the tombstone. You might find information that wasn't included in the transcription.

—*Carrie Taylor*

  QUICK TIPS

Grandma Hid Her Treasures

When my husband's grandmother died, we bought her home. Because of this, only Grandma's very visible possessions were gathered and distributed to family (furniture, photos, etc). The rest of the stuff in the house was left for us to sift through as time permitted. Because we were moving in on top of Grandma's stuff, I had to do a lot of rearranging. I had never before realized the scope of Alzheimer's disease until I began to run across what were probably this woman's most treasured possessions in some of the oddest places. Some of the things were squirreled away in musty, dusty corners, and many things would have been in danger of being thrown away but for my own curiosity. I found cards that her husband had given her over the years hidden between old tablecloths, and the menu from the restaurant where she and her husband had eaten on their wedding day, hidden between some old books in a box destined for the trash. The most amazing find, to me, was the certificates of achievement for Grandma from school and her baptism certificate, which I would not have found if I hadn't felt compelled to read the contents of a newspaper from 1950 that I found in the basement. If the deceased had any kind of dementia before they died, you may have to really look hard for their treasures, because they love to hide things.

—*Jolynn Noel*
Winland, West Virginia

Ask Questions in Family Newsletters

My aunt and I send out a family newsletter every couple of months to let everyone know how we are doing on the family tree. When we do, we ask about a specific memory that family members would remember. For example, my great-grandmother would always say, "Land sakes."

We asked for everyone to let us know what they remembered and in this manner, we found a family treasure. My great-grandfather used a spittoon and called it a "mickey bucket." Everyone remembered it but no one knew where it was. I recently received a letter from my great aunt telling me how she liked the newsletter. In it, she shared a few memories and the fact that she had the copper spittoon. A family treasure found!

—*Bonnie Cousino*

Deciphering an Unknown Language

Have you discovered a stone with an unusual transcription that you believe is written in a foreign tongue and needs translation? Before you jump to that conclusion, consider this inscription that came from an old, partly broken and faded tombstone I was asked to decipher. I realized that some of the unusual-looking characters were just A's and I's. The inscription read:

1745
MARIA OPTIGRAFF B__ <—Missing
BIIN BARIT HIR
THA 3 FA AF
AGOST BIIN ATEN
EARS AF AJH

Previous researchers presumed the inscription was some sort of Dutch or German. I tried to imagine the way a Dutch or German immigrant would say it. AJH resembled AGE. AGOST sounded like AUGUST. BARIT HIR became BURIED HERE. The entire inscription became:

1745
MARIA OPTIGRAFF BORN?
BEING BURIED HERE
THE 3- TH OF
AUGUST BEING EIGHTEEN
YEARS OF AGE

It was just Broken English! Broken English of a "flavor" harmonizing with the nationality of the deceased—not German or Dutch at all.

So whose language is it, anyway? If you stop and think about it, it just might be yours!

—*Vince Summers*

Put a Family Tree on Your Headstone

My grammy (my dad's mom) knew how people liked to trace their family trees. She told us that when she died she wanted us to put her children's names, and the city in which they lived, on the back of her tombstone, We kept this tradition with my mother's parents and I plan on keeping this as a tradition in my own family. Won't this be an interesting way to backtrack some day?

— *Cathy Russell*

Photographing Surnames at the Cemetery

My husband and I have been researching all four lines of our family. We have been through numerous cemeteries in Michigan and Canada, and it seems that we often find a headstone of the person we are looking for, and then another, right behind it, with the same last name. We bring our camera and take photos of all headstones that have any of the last names we are researching.

This does not sound like much, but when we were in Canada in August, we were researching with a distant cousin on my side. We made our way through about eight or more cemeteries, and I have eight rolls of film. I keep these photos in an album, and as I find another ancestor on paper, I go to the book to see if I might have a headstone to match my paper information.

One of the nicest features I found on the Canadian headstones, was that 95% of the time the wife is on the headstone with her maiden name: "wife of (her husband's name)." as I walked through several cemeteries, I found information on women in the family that we could not find any further information for. On one stone, we found Elijah Forsythe, and under that name was Phoebe C. Marlatt, wife of Elijah Forsythe, along with her date of death, and her age. Not having a Phoebe in my generation research list, I took the photo and once I got home, I worked to make that connection.

I find that I have a headstone to match most new names, just from that first trip to Canada. On the next trip, we will concentrate on Marlatts buried near the Niagara Peninsula, around Grimsby, Hamilton, and St. Catherines.

—*Rozann Osborn*

Transfer of Remains

One of my four great-grandfathers owned a bakery on Catherine Street in Manhattan, which he continued to operate after moving to Brooklyn in 1848.

When he moved to Brooklyn, he not only brought his living family, but also the remains of three deceased children. Several years ago, I asked the Green-Wood Cemetery staff about the fact that the first three interments in an old family plot took place on the same date. They checked the records and said that they were removals from the Old Dutch Burial Ground on Houston Street in Manhattan. The Green-Wood staff said that this was a common practice in those days.

It's amazing how popular transfers of remains were. One of my third great-grandfather's sons-in-law was buried in Green-Wood three different times. Another ancestor had the remains of eight different relatives moved within Calvary Cemetery in Queens and all reburied on 14 March 1876.

Researching Green-Wood burial records has really reinforced the importance of getting a complete list of burials from the cemetery instead of relying upon information on headstones. The old plot in Green-Wood only has headstones with the names of about a dozen individuals, including the oldest stones, which are now illegible. The cemetery records show that 57 people were buried in the plot between 1848 and 1983. A contested will from 1874 helped me to identify the relationship of many of the individuals.

—*Kelvin MacKavanag*

Use GPS in Cemeteries

I recommend adding degrees of latitude and longitude when describing the location of a cemeteries and obscure burial sites. Lat/Lon allows pinpointing locations within mere feet. It is especially helpful in finding an accurate location of grave sites in rural areas, many of which are unmarked, overgrown, abandoned, and may only contain one or two graves.

A Global Positioning System (GPS) device can be purchased for well under $100. Pawn Shops are a good source. They're simple and easy to use. Just turn them on at the site you want to record, and within a minute or so the degrees of lat/lon are displayed.

Try it. I believe that in the future, genealogy buffs and other researchers will appreciate this bit of extra effort on our part. I sure wish my ancestors had passed this kind of information on to me.

—*[Unsigned]*

Photograph Cemetery Landmarks

When I go to a cemetery, I not only take photos of tombstones, I also take photos of the church and, if available, photos of pillars or archways that lead into the cemetery. This not only is a landmark for me on my sojourns on tombstone searches, but there may also be information inscribed on a plaque in front of, or on the church, or on the pillars or archways at the entrance. There may be a monument within the cemetery itself with valuable information on it. As for me, I really enjoy looking for evidence of my ancestor's existence and as much information that I can collect when I am in my "in search of" mode, for my unknown ancestors.

—*Laura LaRose,*
Boswell, Pennsylvania

Trouble-Free Cemetery Labels

I take lots and lots of cemetery photos. Here's a tip for trouble-free labeling: I write on a white page on a clipboard, in dark felt tip, the name of the cemetery and the city/state (and location number if there is enough space to write) all clearly and large enough to show up in my photo. Then religiously, I put the card at the base of the monument on either the west or the north position to the marker. I only deal with west or north, so west would be to the left of the monument, and north would be to the right of the monument. Every photo I take is immediately identifiable. I don't need labels or a pen. I can use the photos the second they come out of the photo envelope.

—Valentine

Diagram Headstone Locations

I photograph the entry to the cemetery or the church where a particular headstone is located. I also draw a quick sketch showing the orientation of the cemetery and the location (row and plot) of my ancestor's grave(s). That way, I can find them quickly on any return visit or direct other family members to their location.

—*Ila Verne Toney*
Conroe, Texas

Camera Lens Makes Stone Legible

Recently, I was in a cemetery on a rainy day looking for my ancestors' gravestones. When I found the gravestones, several were difficult to read because of the wear on them with the passing of time and the exposure to bad weather. I wanted to photograph them anyway, and when I put the camera to my eye I discovered that I could make out some of the lettering and numbers on some of the stones a little better than with my naked eye. My husband suggested that it might have something to do with the filtering of light through the lens. I don't know what it was, but it helped me to make out the name Eliza on one particular stone that was badly decayed. Maybe this will work for others, too.

—*Sherry Kilgore*

Cemetery Warning

When you are in a cemetery, is always advisable to pre-set your cell phone to 911 in the event you need to call for police assistance or other emergency. This way one does not have to go about punching numbers, just the send button will get the assistance to you. One of my friends has a business in the more desolate parts of the Viuex Carre of New Orleans. When she must leave late at night or on desolate weekends daylight hours she has her cell phone preset to 000 and laying on the passenger side of her car. Just passing on a great safety idea.

— John Cordero

Note: Since many of us may be visiting cemeteries at this time of year, here are more cemetery tips from last year:

Anyone planning on visiting a cemetery should be especially wary at this time of year. Mother's Day, Memorial Day, and Father's Day see an increase in visitors to the cemetery.

Thieves know this, too. This makes cemetery visitors an appealing target for theft. Whenever you visit the cemetery it's a good idea to follow some common sense safety precautions:

- Don't leave your purse or other valuables in your car.
- If possible, go with a group.
- Go during the daylight hours.
- If you have a cell phone, it is also a good idea to bring it with you so that you can call for help if necessary. Stay safe!

Cemetery Research at a Distance

When some of my cousins moved to Alabama, they visited a churchyard where we have relatives buried. They sent me photos, wherein I noticed a pot of flowers on one of the family plots. This indicated that relatives might be living nearby and caring for the graves. I searched the Internet white pages for family surnames in that town, found several, and wrote to them. The result was a whole batch of new relatives. Other things to look for in photos include freshly cleaned head-stones, veterans' flags, or seasonal items at the gravesites.

—*Nancy Protzman*

Putting a Face with the Tombstone

While I am taking pictures of headstones for our family history book, I include a picture of the person or persons that go with the headstone. It makes it much easier for all of us to remember who Uncle George was if his picture is included.

Also, a plus is that we get to see the clothing that was worn in his day.

—*K.Sullivan*
Michigan

Battle of the Bulge Gravesites

I recently visited the American cemetery in Luxembourg, which contains many of the graves from the Battle of the Bulge. While there, I went to the visitors building and was told that the best way to receive a photo of a grave is to send money for flowers. I am sure the form to use in ordering flowers is available from the Veterans Administration. Orders should reach the overseas offices two months in advance of the desired date. I was told that $30 was an appropriate amount. I am sure I will never be able to visit my uncle's grave in the Philippines but I can have a photo, at least.

— *Norma Wilson*
Golden, CO

Note: More information is on the American Battle Monuments Commission website at <http://www.abmc.gov/abmc5.htm>.

Mark the Grave for Other Visitors

Ever wonder who else visits your ancestors' grave sites? I did, so I placed a brief message about the ancestor, with my name, address, phone number, and the date on a 3x5 card. I put it in a zip lock bag, stapled it to a dowel, and placed it at the grave. I also requested on the card that my "flag" be left at the grave, for others to see. This has worked many times.

—Shirley Penna-Oakes
Rock-n-O Ranch, Tum Tum, WA

Get Grave Details from Local Society

Before you visit the cemetery, call the local Genealogical Society. See if they have the cemetery records for the cemetery you plan to visit. Many times someone will have already copied down the data that is on the tombstones at a much earlier date when the inscriptions were easily readable. They also generally list the divisions of the cemetery, by section and row, thus making it easier for you to find the graves that you are looking for as well as ones that may be related to you that you didn't even know about. Many times the cemetery records will be indexed, making it faster to find the names you are looking for.

Now you can also check out the church records while you're at the Genealogical Society. That could be a treasure trove of baptismal and marriage records as well as details about funerals. Now go visit the cemetery armed with all this information and find your ancestors. While there, look for newer graves that weren't included in the cemetery records at the genealogical society. If the inscription is easy to read, just take a photo. Have a spray bottle of distilled water and brushes with you just in case there's some dirt in the gravestone and some small shears in case the grass is a little to tall for a good photo.

—*Dave*

Reading Cemeteries by Flashlight

Several years ago, my brother and I were behind schedule when we arrived at a cemetery. The sun had gone down, and we had to do our search by flashlight. To our surprise, we found that old, weathered stones were sometimes easier to read by flashlight than they might have been in full sun. The play of light and shadow made the carvings stand out.

—*Loretta Evans*
Idaho Falls, Idaho

What Gravestones Can't Tell You!

Some cemeteries allow only one name on the headstone—that of the deed holder. In my mother's family plot in Calvary Cemetery, Woodside, LI, NY, only the name Egan is on the stone, but the last time I checked, there are fourteen relatives buried in that plot.

Gravestone Legible in the Afternoon

I was astounded to find my husband's great-grandparents' long lost tombstone in the cemetery where I had long been doing research. The cemetery records had been burned by the caretaker who was suffering from Alzheimer's disease, so they weren't available. After searching cemeteries all around and coming up empty, I figured the great-grandparents died so long ago that their tombstone was lost to the ages.

One day, instead of being at the cemetery at my usual 10 **a.m.**, I was there at 3 **p.m.** There in the row behind the many family plots, I caught sight of familiar names on a tombstone that was so old it was "unreadable" in the morning light. I had paid no attention to it before, but this tombstone came to life in the afternoon sun. It was my husband's great-grandparents, and I had one of those jaw-dropping moments. I even learned his great-grandmother's maiden name and their dates of birth. A different time of day or time of year might make all the difference in reading a tombstone.

— Trish

Obituaries in Unexpected Places

When my dad died, I was upset that the newspaper in the next town did not carry his obituary. Then I realized that, in fact, there was a long front-page article about my dad and his various accomplishments and elective positions. If you are checking newspapers yourself, don't just look at the obituary page, particularly if the person you seek was at all well-known in the local area. The death may be classified under "news."

—Kate Randall Reeves
Mountain Center, California

Misinformation from a Non-Resident

While trying to find a town in Nebraska for a cousin-in-law in Washington, I realized something that I had before taken for granted. Doing research at the local museum archives, I noticed that several of the obituaries said the deceased had resided in Garfield, which I knew to be the county precinct where this family lived in the country, not a town. Someone who is not native to the area might not know this.

I found the extinct town I was looking for when a website listed the precincts along with the towns. So the "town" you are looking for may very well be a precinct within the county instead.

—Pat Herrick
Franklin, Nebraska

Tips for an Obituary Search

When looking up or requesting an obituary, I suggest you ask for or look at the newspapers for a day or two prior to the death date. If the death was caused by a newsworthy event, there may be news items that will shed further light on events in the life of the deceased. You should also search the paper for a minimum of two to four days following the publication of the death notice. As I look through the obituary section in our daily paper, I frequently see one or several corrections or additions to obituaries printed earlier. Quite often, this additional information will concern other survivors, correction of dates, or other information not given in the original notice. By taking this extra step you may gain much valuable data for your files.

—Jane Kuck

Vital Records for Future Generations

Be sure to print a loved one's obituary in the town of his birth. Recently, my cousin died in south Florida and the local newspaper wanted an astronomical amount of money to print a basic obituary. The family did not have that much money to spare.

Being a genealogist, I know how important a published obituary can be for future generations, plus I believe that everyone deserves that last hurrah. My first step was to have the obituary published in my hometown's newspaper in West Virginia; the small community newspaper will print them for free. I then called the Brockton Enterprise in Brockton, Mass., the town where my cousin was born, and found that they also printed obits for free. I sent one out. One of my cousin's survivors was a daughter whose whereabouts were unknown. After this obit was printed in the Brockton Enterprise, my cousin's widow received a phone call from that lost daughter, who had been living in Brockton all along. Another cousin found their way through cyberspace to us as a result of reading the obituary.

More than likely, had we been able to print the obit in the Florida paper, we would have never considered printing in the Brockton paper, as my cousin had not lived there for several decades. I will certainly do the same for any other family members that pass away. Bless those newspapers who provide this service free!

—Jolynn Winland

Note: Here are a couple of good sources:
Newspapers.com—*http://www.newspapers.com*
NewsLink—*http://www.newslink.org/menu.html*

—eds.

U.S. Funeral Director Listings

Having done family research for twenty-five years, and having been on staff at local Family History Centers for about twenty years, I have discovered a book that is invaluable for family history research. However, not many researchers seem to have heard of this wonderful resource. It is *The National Yellow Book of Funeral Directors*.

This book lists the funeral homes for the entire United States, along with some cemeteries and newspapers. If I know the city or town that a person lived in when they died, I look in this book to get names and addresses of all the funeral homes in the area. Since it lists their addresses and phone numbers, I contact each one until I find the funeral home that took care of my relative's funeral arrangements. In most cases, they very graciously send me all the information they have for free, which usually will include a copy of the death certificate, the obituary, and additional information about the funeral service. Some thoughtful funeral homes, much to my surprise, have voluntarily sent along all the death information on people who may be related to the person I inquired about. I prefer the older Yellow Books, and they can be found at many funeral homes. They periodically purchase new Yellow Books, and consequently discard the outdated ones. They will give those away for free. The Yellow Books can also be found online from used book distributors.

—*Suzie Ogilvie Sabin*
Shelton, Wash.

Soundex Sounds

I have been looking for years in Massachusetts for earlier records of my ancestor, John W. Buttomer. He is in the 1900 Census as b. Mass. 1848. I searched in indices and whole towns with no results, using Soundex, because I know spelling was inconsistent. Soundex for Buttomer is B356.

One day I decided to vary the spelling to Buttermer, which is Soundex B365 with the extra "r." With the new code, I found him in 1850, in Billerica as Buttermore, with parents Francis and Catherine!!! Birth is one year off, but his parents' first names are the first names of his two children, plus the middle initial W. is present. So, my suggestion is this: don't get tied into one Soundex code. Stick an extra consonant in, especially an "r" in New England! It opened up a whole new generation for me.

—*Carole Williams*

Black History in the Census

In the course of my genealogical wandering, I was studying the 1910 Graham Co. Kansas Census when I stumbled upon some pages of the Nicodemus, Kansas area. I thought it was interesting that in 1910, Nicodemus, Kansas was a fairly large, almost completely black community of farmers. Also, on the same census film was Geary County, Kansas, home of Fort Riley. Fort Riley had a very large population of black military men listed.

—John

The 1910 Census is available as part of Ancestry's Census Subscription package. Census subscribers can view these images by going to <www.ancestry.com/rd/census.htm> and clicking "View Images." Then just click: 1910/Kansas/Graham Co./Nicodemus Or to view Ft. Riley: 1910/Kansas/Geary/OtherTownships/District60-Fort Riley Military Reservation

—Juliana Smith

Four Tips for Census Research

Census indexes are a valuable resource for finding the family you are looking for, but sometimes the family you are looking for seems to be absent from the locale, even when you are certain they were living there. Here are a few strategies for locating them.

1. Look for spelling variations, i.e., Morison, Morrisson, or Merrison for Morrison, or Rause for Rouse. I have one ancient relative that has a different spelling in every census. These variations are often correctly indexed; just spelled different by the census taker.
2. Look for typographical errors. These are misspellings related to keyboard entry— letters out of order. Geroge for George, Willaim for William, Dnaiel for Daniel, etc.
3. Try searching by first name only in the specific locale. The Ancestry search engine will accept this type of search. (Leave the surname field blank.)
4. Try displaying all the names of households in a specific town, or on a specific page, etc.(To do this, leave the name fields blank, and specify the state, county, town or page number.) This also works for finding related families. Of course, you can page through the town and read the names of the people who lived there using the actual image pages, but with a slow connection, it can take a while, and if the names are hard to read, looking at the list of indexed names may be helpful.

—G.A. Rouse

Did She Lie about Her Age?

If you are having trouble finding the marriage date of a couple who had only daughters and are basing the date of marriage for the parents on the ages of the daughters in adulthood, keep in mind that the daughters may have lied about their ages. I had this problem and based the marriage year of the parents of five daughters on their respective ages given in the 1900 census. Well, the daughters had all lied about their ages by up to five years. They probably learned that trick from their mother who also lied about her age by five years.

Once I deduced their real ages I had no problem locating the parent's marriage record.

—Bobby

Deciphering Census Names

For those times when you can't read the last name on a census record, I have found that if you put in the state, county, and township in the index search engine without a name, all the names of the people in the township appear in alphabetic order. Just scroll down to the first letter of the last name and see if you can find how to spell the person's name. Right now this would work for the 1790-1870, 1920, and 1930 censuses at Ancestry.com.

—Jane Joukema
Denver, CO

Print Index on Reverse of Images

When you find someone in a census index, go to the printer-friendly page, and print that page. Using the information from the index, locate the individual in the census images. Now, make your next print of the census image on the backside of the previous print The result is a census image on one side, and the information from the index on the other side of the page.

To save ink, try printing in Draft. This will save you a lot of ink and is still very readable.

—*Donald G. Banhart*
Portland, Oregon

Family Secrets behind the Census

When you find a family in the census, be sure to check out the name of the census taker at the top of the page. I did this and found that one of my ancestors was the census taker. Just a little extra info to add to your family history—an ancestor who was a census taker.

—*Susan J. Fevola*

Last Name Recorded as First Name

I have been searching for my wife's great-grand-father for several years but to no avail. I received the complete set of the 1880 United States Census and National Index for Christmas and thought that surely I would find him there. However, I still found nothing. After trying every possible spelling variation of his surname, I finally tried entering his first name as his last name, and his last name as his first name, BINGO, there he was. His whole family, but with the wrong last name.

—*Lee*
Spokane

Find Your Relative's Neighbors

Sometimes the census indexes can be frustrating. I was searching for my uncle, Jacob Michelstein, in Newark, New Jersey, with no results. Then I remembered that I had copies of the city directory for the years 1910-30. Most of these were just the alphabetical listings, but I also had one for Johnson Avenue in 1923, showing that his family and my other aunt (his wife and her sister) lived two doors apart. By using the names of the neighbors listed in 1923, I finally found my uncle and his family.

—Barbara Zimme

Census Checkoff Sheet

Whenever I start researching a new family, I like to obtain all the census records in which each family member may appear. I created a "Census Checkoff" sheet in *Excel*. The headings on the columns are labeled: Name, Born, 1850, 1860, 1870, 1880, 1900, 1910, 1920, 1930, and Died.

I start off with the name of the head of the family. The next column is for the date the person was born. This makes it easier to quickly see when a person would first enter the census. This column is followed by each census year, as listed above, then the year the person died. Putting the "Died" column at the end helps you to see the last census this person would have been in. If you know the date, you can put an "X" in this last census year. I put enough rows on each sheet to hold about twenty people, which should cover the largest family size. I adjust the rows and col-umns where needed to make small notes. In each square, where the census year intersects with the name of the individual, I might put a small note for events in his or her life. For example, I put an "M" for married or "D" for died.

I first started just making notes on a sheet of paper but found that by making this form in *Excel* I have one standard to use for all my families. This helps to see trends in a family's history, e.g., if several young children are missing in an individual year, this may point to an epidemic or illness in an area. Or if several older children are missing from the family, this may be a signal that the children married and may have moved to another area together since families tended to migrate together.

—*Rhonda Dunn*

Posting SS-5 Information Online

Like many others, I've ordered my share of Social Security Forms SS-5 in the quest to construct my family tree. Several of the forms turned out to be of people who seem to be unrelated—so far.

These forms have information that may be valuable to someone else who finds the cost of ordering the SS-5 forms prohibitive. I've added the genealogical information to The Ancestry World Tree for each of the SS-5 forms I've acquired. This provides a three-person tree—the applicant, and the applicant parents, as well as the birth date and place of the applicant. None of this many seem very important, but that information may just provide the necessary clues to break someone else's brick wall. If that someone contacts me, I can give them the employment and residence information on the form. I hope, too, that some kind soul out there has a bit of the information I'm searching for, and posts their unrelated SS-5s to the Ancestry World Tree. Be still my impatient heart!

—*Dawn Dixon*

Another great way to share this information is by using the new "User Comments" feature on Ancestry.com. Just locate the entry in the SSDI and click on the User Comment link (with the little post-it icon) on the right hand side of the screen. A pop-up window will then appear and you can post the additional information right with the entry so that others who run across it will be able to see your comments along with the entry.

—*eds.*

 QUICK TIPS

Random Acts of Genealogical Kindness

When you come across names from the distant past in magazines and other publications, post the basic information—names, dates, source, etc.—to message boards or other online sites so that others may fill in some gaps in their research. This is especially important for African-Americans who often have difficulties tracing their ancestry before 1870.

I just read a magazine article about a black man who was born a slave around 1850 and went on to become a top horse trainer. I posted his name, his estimated birth year, the state in which he lived, and the source of the information to a message board that is dedicated to African-American genealogy.

The article contains much more information about his life and mentions another black horse trainer. Because I cited the source of the informa-tion, any of the descendants can get a copy of the full article from the library or by contacting the magazine for a back issue.

—Diana

Sharing a City's Centennial Book

I found an old centennial book for Ellsworth, Iowa, in a thrift store and bought it for a dollar because my husband is from Iowa. None of his family's names were listed in it, but it had a wealth of information with pictures of families, homes, businesses, and school classes. It told about the founding of this area and had lists of church congregations and various clubs.

I looked for Ellsworth Historical or Genealogical Society, but could find none. So I looked on the message boards at Ancestry.com and found people who were looking for connections in Ellsworth, Iowa. From that, I chose the person who had the most family names, someone whose families were pioneers there and helped establish it. I e-mailed him and he said he had been looking for that book. I asked him to please help others with it. It cost under $2 to send by book post.

I'm urging you to help others in this way, and to also check libraries for centennial books. They are a wonderful resource.

—Laraine Hall
Camarillo, California

  QUICK TIPS

Envelopes Provide Useful Information

I learned this the painful way: Keep the envelopes that letters come in, not just the letters! We recently discovered a trunk-full of old family letters, but many had no envelope—and therefore, no date/place to start looking. The ones with envelopes propelled us right along.

—*Mona*

A Business Card for Conferences

I would like to suggest that genealogy conference attendees make up business cards on their computers with their name, address, telephone number (optional), e-mail address, and area of research or interest to carry with them to any genealogy meeting or conference. This way, attendees can share personal information with other attendees they wish to keep in contact with. An alternative is to make a Word document, several on a page, with the information, to cut into small handouts. I have attended many business conferences and have made many contacts, exchanged business cards and kept in contact with these people. I would make a note on the back of each card I received to remind me who was who when I got home, the topic of information exchanged, etc.

—*Marge Clark*

Check Ship Lists for Non-Immigrants

Even if you know your family did not immigrate to the United States through Ellis Island, check the database anyway <http://www.ellisislandrecords.org>. I have found many collateral relatives, some more than once, returning to the U.S. from vacations and business trips.

—*Annette Fulford*

Bibles on eBay

I don't know if this has been brought up before, but to find some of the best information of family trees would be to check out the family bibles on eBay. I was quite surprised at the different surnames I came across by searching the old family bibles. Most families kept everything written down in the family Bibles.

—*Brenda Roberts*

Double Check Sources

I have a lovely photo of my great grandmother's gravestone, which is very detailed. It gives the names of her parents, her husband and where and when she was born. It states she was born on 4 February 1873 and she departed this life on 25 June 1933. But when I actually obtained copies of her birth and death records, she was born in 1875 and died on 24 June. (She was buried on 25 June 1933.) Do not assume the information is correct, just because it is carved in stone.

—*Annette Fulford*
British Columbia, Canada

Check Under "U" for "Unknown"

When searching alphabetical indexes for my family surnames, I always check under "U" for listings recorded as "Unknown." Sometimes the surname might be recorded as "unknown" but the given name, relevant date or other information might match the person or family you're looking for.

—*Laura Mackinson*
St. Louis, Missouri

Marking Your Place on Microfilm

When I must use a reader to scan the roll of microfilm and then move the roll to a microfilm printer, it can be difficult to find the same spot easily and quickly. Recently, I discovered a great way to mark my place on a roll of microfilm using only a small piece of paper. I take a small piece of paper—about half an inch by three inches—and insert it into the reel of microfilm before I re-wind it. When I take it to the printer, I can wind quickly to the spot I need.

This is especially helpful if I find several places on the same roll of film that need prints.

— *M. La Nell Shores*
Oklahoma City

Finding New Genealogy Resources

After all but exhausting the possibilities at the local library, I started wondering where else I could find more ancestor references and data. Then, I realized there are several used bookstores nearby. Sure enough, each one had whole sections of genealogical books. They just happened to pile up, since as it seems to me, there are only two or three of us in the area who actually actively try to look up our ancestry.

Also, one night while surfing the Web, I started wondering what those P2P programs do, other then swap MP3 files. I found three extensive family trees that related to my family. These were of three of my eight great-grandmothers. I had been searching for them for years. What a find they were!

—*Brian*

Brigham Young University has set up a P2P site for genealogy at:
http://genealogy.byu.edu/index.jsp

—*eds.*

County Maps

This summer while on a cemetery finding trip to Barbour County, West Virginia, I stopped by the courthouse and bought a county map. It has cemeteries, dirt roads, small streams and apparently all buildings including churches and schools charted on the map. The local library had a book giving directions to the cemeteries and listings of burials. I was able to compare the directions with the map and locate cemeteries I know I would have otherwise missed. I labeled my map and now have a record so I can find my way back on future trips.

—*Janice Burner Humphreys*
Lansing, Kansas

Printing on Photo Paper

Whether you are planning a research trip or just printing out information that you will be referring to constantly, try printing it on photo paper. The image will be sharp and clear with darker print, and the paper, being a bit stiffer, will hold up to sustained use. This works particularly well with both old and new maps.

—Dorothe Conrey Turley
Palos Verdes Peninsula, California

Colored Paper and Microfilm

Our Family History Center keeps several sheets of colored paper available to be used with the microfilm readers. If the background is "murky," try putting a piece of colored paper on the viewing surface. The paper filters out the murkiness and enhances the images. Surprisingly, this often works very well. Light gray and light blue seem to work best, but other colors to try would be bright pink and bright yellow. You never know what might work with your particular microfilm so don't be afraid to experiment.

I have started including a few sheets of colored paper in my notebook when I visit libraries, archives, etc. to be used for this purpose. There is nothing worse than having a microfilm that you can't read!

— *Beth Manchester*

Archival-Safe Page Protectors

We've heard about using archival-safe paper, but many still don't know that plastic page protectors also need to be archival-safe. When selecting page protectors or photo protector sheets, remember the "Three Pollys." These include polyester, polyethylene, and polypropanol. These are archival-safe materials. If the package or your vendor can't verify the content of the materials, don't buy the product.

—Mary Clement Douglass, CGRS
Former Museum Curator
Salina, Kansas
www.historical-matters.com

Indexing All of Your Genealogy Files

Like most genealogists, I had a file system that was not in good order, to say the least. I finally decided to do something about it, since papers that I copied to send to others sometimes never made it back to the correct files.

My solution was to go through each file, list every piece of paper in the file in order, and print the list as an index. I stapled this list to the inside of the file folder. I keep the master list in a "Contents of Files" document and can refer to it when I am looking for a particular bit of information, without pulling all the file folders out. If some new information is added to a file it is easy to add it to the index for that file and print a new index.

—Nadine Wilson

"Around to It" Website Folder

I have often-times found myself reading about a new site to check out on the Web. Usually this has happened when I do not have the time. You know what I mean—when I am stealing a few minutes and really should be doing something else in the first place. Recently, I came up with an idea to keep track of these sites. I have created a new folder in my "favorites" (or bookmarks).

I marked this folder "around-to-it." You know, when you get "around to it" you will have another look. Well it works great. When I get the chance I go back and look at the site, then file it away appropriately to use in the future.

—*Karen Kelly Kiss*

Keeping Family Lines Straight

Sometimes, when I am referring to a new family group, I have to ponder a bit about with which line the family belongs. This is especially true of new, young families and new surnames. I have begun writing the name of the ancestor in the upper right hand corner of the family group sheet. This way, I can tell immediately which line the family belongs to. This is a good reminder and a good time saver.

—*Marjorie Rouse*
Iowa

Citing Books

When researching at a library or wherever I make a copy from a book, I write on the back of the copy (in pencil) the name of the library and city and state where I made the copy. I also copy the title page and make a note of the reference place at the library. Then if I have to "prove" my source to someone, I have it handy.

—*Iris F. Harris*

Save Time with Pre-Punched Paper

I got in the habit of hole punching the paper that came out of my printer until I went to an office supply store one day to buy printer paper. I discovered there is a company (Willamette) that has paper conveniently punched with the three holes. Now, when I know I will be filing research into the family notebook I use this paper, and when I am filing to other sources, I use unpunched paper. The price is the same for both types of paper.

—*Charee R.*

Genealogy Rolodex

I have found that the easiest way to keep track of e-mail addresses is to keep a Rolodex wheel next to my computer. My friends all have cards in it, with their name, address, phone, and e-mail close at hand.

For genealogy, each family surname also has a card or cards with a listing of the e-mail addresses of the people I have corresponded with online who are also researching that surname. I also include a keyword or two about their search.

When I receive a bonanza, such as a careful listing of all the graves and headstones for one of my surnames in a major cemetery in Galway, Ireland, I can share that information easily with all the researchers I have met online, who might have use for some part of that information, because I have all their information near at hand on my cards for that surname.

When I finally find what I think is a link to one or two of them, I can e-mail joyously with my new information—without having to look through files or "file piles."

In addition, right there at my fingertips, my Rolodex contains a card for each genealogy membership, genealogy subscription, and genealogy vendor I have used, including 800 phone numbers, mail addresses, e-mail addresses, dates of subscription and memberships, etc.

—*Maureen Shelly*

Insert a Blank Page When Scanning

I use my scanner quite a bit, as well as the commercial copiers available at most public libraries, and have had copies sent to me. One thing you need to keep in mind when using these wondrous devices: Unless you put a blank page behind the one you are copying, you risk the chance of print from the opposite side appearing on the page you wish to copy (just as if you had held it up to the window). This is especially true of handwritten documents where there is frequently greater ink penetration than with printed material. These "bleed-throughs" can make the already difficult task of transcribing seventeenth; and eighteenth-century documents increasingly difficult. It takes little time to slip a blank page in behind the one you are copying, and the result will be a clear, clean copy.

—*Judith Schwab*

Is the Boarder a Family Member?

In census records, many households will have individuals enumerated as "boarders." Don't dismiss these people as strangers. Often they are family members and the surname may give a clue about a married woman's maiden name, or a little searching of that name may reveal another branch of the family. In the 1930 census, in the household of my in-laws, a George Pritchard is listed as a "boarder." In reality, he was the brother of my husband's grandmother, who also lived in the home. And of course, his surname was the maiden name of the grandmother. Sometimes, young men will be listed as boarders and turn out to be brothers of the wife.

I have also seen circumstances where parents of the wife will be referred to as boarders. Check it out—you might find a chink in that brick wall!

—*Kathy Dixon*
Newbury, Ohio

Use Expandable Files

As genealogical files grow, you need a way to expand your filing system. I found a quick, easy, inexpensive, and effective solution. My documents are placed in folders labeled with the relevant person's name and date of birth. Folders are then sorted alphabetically in expandable file pockets. Each pocket is numbered. I then create an index using *Excel*. Each line shows the folder title, a brief description of contents, and the expandable pocket number.

As the files grow, I just add expansion pockets, move the files, and update the index. Finding a file is as easy as locating the name on the index and locating the appropriate expansion pocket. The *Excel* index keeps track of everything as the files grow and move from pocket to pocket. *Excel* can sort the index by pocket number and last name.

—*Alan Phelps*

Keeping Track of Genealogy Contacts

Like most genealogy buffs, I correspond by e-mail with a lot of people who are researching the same family lines as myself. When I add a New Contact to my e-mail Address Book, I use "genealogy" as the category and the family name in place of the company name. This makes it easier to send the new information to those interested in my mother's side of the tree and not those on my dad's mother's side.

—*El Dena Ferrell*

Magnetic Bulletin Board

I suggest making your own magnetic bulletin board for your family history space. Decide what you want to be magnetic—a board, plywood, picture backing, frame with backing, etc. Buy magnetic paint—yes they make it. Read directions well and prepare your work area carefully. Tape neatly around your item to contain the thick paint and not paint it onto things around it. Takes two coats—the second added after first coat has been dry for twenty-four hours. It may have smallish lumps in it, smooth them on your surface the best you can—it is iron filings.

When finished, remove the tape and place it or hang it wherever you want it. The whole surface will be magnetic. You can buy very small powerful magnets to supplement, use regular ones, or just use items that will adhere to your magnetic surface.

You no longer have to worry about putting tacks through your precious pictures, charts, or maps, etc, and you can remove and replace items so easily. I saw this idea on Martha Stewart's program.

— *Norma Hurley*

Save Newsletters for Future Research

As I read each day's *Ancestry Daily News*, I edit the newsletter and delete what I don't need to save. In the title, I add small quick notes in parentheses of the items saved so I don't have to peruse each one to find the one I want to research further on. Example: *Ancestry Daily News*, 12 Oct 2001 (Legacy docs)

—*Bob Braunhardt*

Find Helpful Maps on Topozone.com

I couldn't locate some of my maternal ancestors in St. Patrick's cemetery in McAdoo, PA, prior to about 1902. McAdoo lies in Schuylkill County. It seemed odd that the church would spring up in such an old area. I posted to message boards on Ancestry for Schuylkill Co., and received a reply from someone stating that St. Patrick's used to be in Audenreid, until a mine caved in under the church. I took it at face value when he said Audenreid was in Luzerne County but I couldn't find a trace of Audenreid in that county.

Then I found a wonderful website, <www.topozone.com>, and I entered McAdoo, Pennsylvania, into their search engine. I received a map showing that McAdoo is actually in a corner of the county right next to Luzerne and Carbon counties, and that Audenreid was to the east in Carbon County! I found the old church cemetery and some of the relatives that were missing their date of death! Topozone has wonderful maps that help me understand the terrain my ancestors lived in. By printing the maps and showing them to my mother, she has remembered little bits and pieces about who lived where, etc.

—Cindy Whited

Digital Cameras at the Library

I enjoyed Della Steckler's Quick Tip related to using a digital camera. I use my digital camera on a regular basis at the Clayton Center for Genealogical Research and the Texas & Local History Collection—both special collection libraries of the Houston (Texas) Public Library System. I use the digital camera to take photos of material on the microfilm reader for censuses, books, maps, city directories, newspapers, etc.

Houston Public Library has no restrictions for using digital cameras in the library, but you should check with the library staff to determine the local rules for your community or libraries you are visiting.

—Lynna Kay Shuffield

Photo Restoration Site

I'm a creative director and Web designer with a growing compulsion for genealogy, and I've just completed a website with two special sections which may be of interest. One is an interactive reconstruction of an extensive nineteenth century family photo album, and the other is a detailed tutorial for non-professionals on digital restoration of antique family photos.

There is no commercial purpose for the site, only a personal interest and an offer of good information.

—Russell P. Granger
http://www.screengenes.com

Photo Labeling Tips

When faced with labeling a large group photo, where individuals may not be lined up in neat rows, here is one solution I've hit upon.

- Put the photo in an archival sheet protector.
- Using an archival pen (fade proof, water proof, acid free -I find mine at art supply stores), draw an oval or circle around each face.
- Number each person, placing the number where it can be seen against clothing or background, but not on the face.
- On a separate sheet of acid free paper, make a list of the numbers and, next to them, where available, the names of known people.
- If you don't know everyone, but want to share the photo with others who may be able to help, make quality scanned or color laser copies of the photo and hand copy another sheet protector. When labeling any photo, I use hints I learned from a rare book librarian. In addition to using an archival pen, she told me never to write in the area behind the faces and to try to choose a dark area of the photo. Then, should the ink somehow manage to migrate through the paper, even though it shouldn't if it is archival, it will not bleed through to such a distracting or important part of the picture.

Another possibility is to put the information on acid free paper and then to tape it to the photo using archival tape.

—*Susan Hopkins*

Labeling Group Pictures

I scan the picture into a photo program that allows notations. Then, I label each person either above the head or on the clothing, in a contrasting color. Many programs allow changing the font direction to vertical, which helps. It's amazing how small you can make the font and still have clarity. I then print the photo on inexpensive archival paper and place it in the album facing the photo. If economy is an issue, print in back and white, or gray tone.

—*Gail Garwood*

Infrared Film and Other Photo Tips

Ever checked out an old family cemetery, house site, or property and found nothing to see or photograph—no markers, foundations, indentations, or indications of occupancy? If so, pictures taken with a camera loaded with infrared film will capture details not visible to the naked eye or that cannot be seen on photographs shot with regular film. Worn lettering on old tombstones, lost gravesites, and buried building foundations will show up on infrared pictures due to decayed man-made organic compounds at the site. These materials, having rotted, alter the natural vegetative pattern and details of human occupation (although blurry) become visible on infrared pictures.

Alternatively, take pictures with regular film late in the afternoon when the sun is low and shadows are long. Collapsed gravesite and foundation locations will show up as square or rectangular areas of shadow. Look for right angles since nature doesn't generally like straight lines.

Two things to note when taking either infrared or regular photographs. First, make sure to have a reference point, e.g., a fence post, a road sign or a natural outcropping included in any pictures taken, infrared or regular film, so that an area photographed can be easily located. Second, change perspective if you are shooting regular film. Standing on a hillock, the bed of a truck, or even a stepladder will allow shadow details to be more readily observable.

—Jerry Plat

Check the Backs of Photos for Clues

When you turn over those old photos, look beyond the names of people in the photo appearing there. There may also be the name and location of the film developer, as well as the date the film was developed. This information can help identify the people in the picture.

My late father had a nephew close to the same age as himself. I have a family photo in which the two are standing next to each other when they were about twelve years old and they look very much alike. In a different photo, there is a young man who could be either of them. When I looked at the back of the photo, I noticed that the film was developed in a small town in California's Central Valley in the 1930s. Since I know that my father visited California the first time in 1956, it told me that this young man was my cousin rather than my father. Sometimes these small clues can save time and prevent confusion.

—*MaryAnn Thurmond*

Creating a Scrapbook for Mother

My mother never told us much about her childhood years, so for her eightieth birthday I decided to create a scrapbook of her life. I asked relatives and friends to send me anecdotes relating to my mother, plus any pictures they might have. One of her sisters sent me many funny memories about my mother and provided pictures as well. If it hadn't been for this sister's memories, I would not have known much about my mother's childhood. Thankfully, I did this! This particular sister passed away less than a year after I created the scrapbook.

Cousins sent their favorite memories; friends sent cards. I devoted a page to each. I was even able to get my mom to tell me about her memories of her grandparents—after showing her some pictures and asking her about them (without her knowing what I was up to). I presented the scrapbook to her as we celebrated her birthday. It is a memory book that will last well past her time and one that will tell future generations what her life was like.

—*Linda Whitman*

Document Your Family Heirlooms

So that our sons will know the stories about our family "treasures," I have photographed each item and written a story about its source. The pictures and stories are kept in a three-ring binder in clear, acid-free sheet protectors. The title is "Where Did It Come From, Mom?" It covers everything from pictures of my grandmother's pump organ to dishes that belonged to my great-great-grandmother. A second set is also in our safety deposit box.

—Marilyn Larson

"Grandma Remembers" Book

I made "Grandma Remembers" books for my teenage grandchildren for Christmas last year. I started with photos of my great grandparents and what I knew of them, then went on to wedding pictures of my grandparents and photos of their home. This continues down the generations, to my parents, then myself, then my children. The photos encompass all stages of their lives, and include my memories of these events and other pertinent events. I also wrote about things we didn't have then that we have now and an eight-generation family tree. They all loved it.

—Granny Geri

House Scrapbook

The owner of the house I am moving into had a great idea and one I plan to emulate. She created a scrapbook of their house. When we first went to look at the house, she had it out and invited us to take a peek. Not only did it show the improvements they had made to the house over the years, but it also included decorations they put up for various holidays, the cabinets she had hand painted, and all the special touches that went in to making that house their home. Now that they are moving on to a new house, it will serve as a record for her family of their first childhood home.

When I wrote the article about "Treasures in My Home," many people wrote to remind me to make a walk through with the video camera to record our house as it was in the "pre-boxes" days. I did this and also took some stills. With the stills, I will create a scrapbook for my daughter of the first house she lived in, as well as making sure the camera is available on moving day to start the next chapter of our lives in our new home.

—*Juliana Smith*

Sharing Copies of Research Offsite

About five years ago, my cousin's house burned down while she and her husband were at work. Unfortunately, they lived in the country so by time the neighbors realized her house was on fire, it was too late. When the fire department got there the house was already gone. There was nothing left to put out but the smoldering embers.

The sad part is that they lost their home. The part that broke my cousin's heart was that fifty years of genealogical research, documents, one-of-a-kind pictures, etc., were gone. No other family member had copies of the information. Everyone in the family would give these things to her and not worry about "what ifs?"

Today, all the genealogy nuts in the family have copies of everything the rest has. We make sure that we each retain the information that we have worked long and hard to replace, so it does not go up in smoke again. Each of us has backup copies somewhere besides at home, just in case.

The good from all of this is that it has brought distant cousins closer together. This year we had our first family reunion. It was wonderful and we met family we never knew existed—including the great-grandchildren of our great-grandfather's siblings. Always share with family members and make sure that others retain copies of what they send you. You never know what can happen.

— *T. Bush*

Protect Your Data from Power Surges

As a reminder and in addition to the ancestry newsletter, you may want to remind readers how important it is to back up their family trees and photos. It isn't enough to protect your computer from power surges; you should also be protecting your cable modem from power surges. There is a simple device, available at Radio Shack for approx $20 that will protect your cable modem from power surges that will destroy(all caps) your hard drive.

Over the Christmas holiday (when we weren't even home!) a power surge came through our cable modem and fried our hard drive. My Gateway is under warranty so I received a new hard drive free of charge. But warranties don't cover lost digital pictures of children and grandchildren, family files, etc.

—*Mary Collins*

Online Storage Space

To add an additional layer of safety for valuable records, not just genealogy files but copies of wills, insurance papers, etc., rent some online storage space. Most sites offer good rates and easy-to-use software.

That way, you can back up all your valuable records and scanned photos away from your home or office. There is no need to buy an expensive safe or fireproof file cabinet. As an added bonus, you can access these records from any computer, anywhere you travel. This is quite handy if you use a laptop to record data.

Some sites for offline storage are:

http://www.xdrive.com/index.cfm
http://www.mydocsonline.com/
http://briefcase.yahoo.com/

Here is a site that lists many more sites for backup data:
http://useful.webwizards.net/wbfs.htm

Archiving Your Information

Many researchers create a permanent record of the information that they have collectedby simply printing it on their computer's printer and then have the record bound. There are a number of snags to this method.

First, modern paper is bleached and the dried bleach turns into acid because of atmospheric moisture. This destroys the paper fibers, so the paper begins to degrade. You've all have seen the yellow color of old newspapers or old paperback books. Paper degradation is easily overcome, because most good stationers can obtain archive quality paper for you. This paper is not bleached, so it does not degrade.

The second problem the permanent record maker encounters is degrading ink. Archive-quality ink is available for dip pens and will work in fountain pens. Printer's ink is also fairly permanent, but it can only be used with lead type or even with rubber stamps. Proper stamping ink is permanent, but these days, we want to print information that we have stored on computer files, so we would want to print it on our personal printers. Inkjet printers use impermanent water-based inks. Laser printers and electrostatic printers use inks based on carbon black, which is stuck to the paper using melted wax. This method is even less permanent. I do not know of any archive quality links which are suitable for a computer's companion printer.

—Adrian Hanwell

Photo Pocket Pages

As I have been scanning my parents' and grand-parents' old photo albums, the albums and pages have been crumbling. A lot of the photos have writing on the back which I don't want to obscure and most of the pictures are small, odd sizes. The standard 4"x6" and 3"x5" photo pockets are a waste of un-used space and the pictures slide around in them, which can't be good for these old photos. One lady mentioned to me that she uses pages designed to hold baseball cards to hold her funeral home cards. While I accompanied my son to his local card shop, I decided to do the same for the few funeral home cards I have. Until then I didn't realize how many different sizes and shapes those pocket pages come in. I found pages that fit my postcards so everyone can read the dates and messages, my tiny old photos, my funeral home cards, and several other odd-sized items that had writing on both sides. Most of the baseball card pocket pages are made with the same archival standards that we look for.

—*Karen Williams*

Taking Care of Old Documents

When you find any old documents that are held together with paper clips, rubber bands, staples, etc., to remove these offending fasteners. Then buy quality archive containers to store these documents—old shoeboxes will not do!

While they hold the letter or document together for now, over a period of thirty years, they start to eat into the original document, leaving nasty marks and blemishes. After one hundred years, the decay gets worse, and after two hundred years, nothing exists unless proper precautions are taken.

My family still holds a number of documents in their private archives, dating from the late 1600s onwards. There are over 2,000 letters from that time until the late 1800s, wills from the 1670s+, samplers, sermons, account books, diaries, etc. My family has recently invested a large amount of money in trying to preserve these documents, but unfortunately some have been subject to visible decay caused by unsuitable paper fasteners and vermin.

I am currently trying to digitize all our records, some of which I now have online. Even transcripts help future generations read now decaying letters or awkward scripts.

Please respect your heritage and remember that money spent now will preserve these documents for future generations. Cash spent now may seem a lot, but what price is heritage?

—*C.R.M.Harrison*
Mullens Harrison Family Archive

Handling 3" x 4" Negatives

Earlier this year I inherited my mother's collection of photos and negatives. I have been scanning them and creating discs for family. In the collection was a group of old negatives (1910-1920). The photo shop in my small town can only handle negatives smaller than 1.5" x 2" and some of my negatives were 3" x 4". The photo shop suggested a local man with a dark room, but the number of negatives I had would make that option too costly.

I decided to try scanning the negatives on my scanner. I scanned them at high resolution then used my photo software to invert (negative) the image and adjust the contrast. While I know that the high light of the scanner is not good for the negatives, this enabled me to see who was in the photos, make fairly clear copies at a reasonable cost, and select those photos that I would like to have professionally printed. This did not work with small negatives, but it woked wonderfully on the ones the photo shop could not print.

—*Kandi*

Protect Oversize Documents

I found a wonderful tip for oversize documents from a mailing list I used to be on. I use oven-cooking bags for all papers that are too large for regular acid-free plastic pages. These cooking bags come in two or three different sizes and are also acid-free.

I also save a lot of the Ancestry Quick Tips and put them in a binder of genealogy tips for easy reference. It has been very helpful. Thanks for all the help over the years.

—Joyce Oelke

Passport Records

If the Ellis Island site shows multiple entries for your ancestors, try looking for them in the Passport Applications Index, using the FHL films. Then, order the appropriate files. It is fascinating to learn of their reasons for traveling back and forth to Europe. Often, other records are attached. If you are lucky, the application photograph may help you with identifying people in photographs, and some family secrets may also be divulged!

—Ann Shaw

Post Office Names

Rememter that the place where the mail was delivered might not be the name of a town. For example, "Potter's Store, Alabama" might actually be a store owned by Mr. Potter, the postmaster in an area where there was no incorporated town; or "Potter's Crossing" could be the crossroads where the post office was located, and not the name of a town.

In the olden days, there were many little "crossroads" in rural areas that are now parts of larger towns and major cities in Europe as well as North America.

Today, we also find that postal delivery areas frequently cross the boundaries from what is now one suburban town and go into the next suburban town, because the delivery areas for the post offices were mapped out when the land between towns was just open country belonging to neither town. And so those residents of Summit may now have mail addresses and zip codes for Evanstown, or vice versa.

Mail addresses to not need to correspond to legal addresses or to town boundary lines. Today, as centuries ago, "city" or "town" on the mailing address simply indicate the name or location of that post office which was assigned many years ago to handle the mail for the particular piece of land in question—no matter what town it is in. Likewise, if your post office should close, your mail will be sent to another post office in another town for delivery to you, and it had better have the correct name and zip code for that post office, never mind the town in which you reside!

—*E. Shelly*

Check Ellis Island Anyway

Haven't checked the Ellis Island database <http://www.ellisisland.org> yet? Do you think your ancestors came earlier, so they didn't stop there? That's what I used to think until I checked the registry on a whim and found thirteen entries for the surname I was researching. Though the family had not immigrated during the time Ellis Island was in operation, they took several trips abroad coming through Ellis Island when returning home and some of the family were even crew members on the ship. One man was listed three times as a crewmember on different ships. Don't be afraid to check different registries even though you think they weren't there.

—*Sherida Childers*

Soundex on the Internet

I thought of this quick tip when I was reading Juliana Smith's "Search Strategy" column in the 6 May 2002 *Ancestry Daily News*.

Some time ago I downloaded a freeware Soundex generator (dated 1994). I have used it on occasion. I figured there might be newer and better ones out there, so I used Google.com to search for Soundex. I found several online Soundex generators, including this one at RootsWeb.com:

<http://resources.rootsweb.com/cgi-bin/soundexconverter>

Or go to the RootsWeb.com home page and select Soundex Converter under their "Tools and Resources." When a result is displayed, it also lists all names it has with the same Soundex code. I used my maternal grandmother's maiden name, Dwyer, since Ms. Smith used the same name. The code is D600, and they list twenty-two names with the same Soundex code.

I also found a freeware downloadable Soundex generator, with a few extra features. It's called ShowSoundex. The link to download it is:

<http://www.sog.org.uk/cig/software/index.html>

The author is Barney Tyrwhitt-Drake. His webpage has a summary of its features:

<http://www.tdrake.demon.co.uk/soundex.htm>

It can handle two names at a time, and has an option of from three to seven characters of Soundex results.

— *Tom McGourin*

Translating Double Consonants

I was intrigued that a nineteenth-century Pennsylvania German ancestor whose name was Weidenhammer was listed in a city directory of the day as Weidenhamer (one "m"). A reference librarian at a historical society explained how this came about when she was shown a photograph of the ancestor's tombstone. The name on the stone was Weidenhamer with a line over the "m." She said this line was commonly used with German surnames to indicate a double consonant. So when the ancestor signed the directory form, he must have written Weidenhamer with a line over the "m." Transcribed by the typesetter into English, the name appears misspelled.

—Patty Mertz
Nashville, Tennessee

Search for Ancestral Homes

If you have an ancestor that lived in a home with a particular title, such as "New Hall, Sussex, England," it may be worthwhile to do a search on the name of the home itself. I did this for two of my ancestors and found pictures of their homes (Loddon Hall and Blickling Hall), portraits of my ancestors, and details about their lives. It turned out that their homes are part of the National Trust in England, and that both ancestors had held prominent positions in the governments of their day. This gave me even more places to look for information on these same ancestors. So try it—you never know what you might turn up!

— *Tita Wyatt*

Check and Recheck Webpages

Recheck databases for family members. They're always growing. I was convinced I had found everything Ancestry.com had on my one particular ancestor. I had checked 100 times and only found snippets. Well, I rechecked two weeks ago and found something new on an updated database. Thanks, Ancestry.com!

I never keep track of what websites I go to. If it is helpful, I bookmark or print it. The Internet changes so quickly, you might miss something.

—*Bradley Marchant*

Creating Timelines with MS Project

I used project management software (such as MS Project) to create a genealogical timeline with associated research tasks. It is convenient since it is both time- and task-oriented. An individual's life can be depicted in a Gaant Chart view as a series of "task bars" with milestones. Milestones are specific events such as birth, marriage, children, and death. Each is depicted on the chart with a specific symbol (typically a triangle). Periods of time for things such as residence, military service, or profession can be shown as task bars, end-to-end or overlapping. Research tasks can be another set of milestones or task bars that can be made to appear below the "lifeline" and can be associated with specific events. This part of the chart is useful as a research log to track your objectives.

You can create a separate "project" for an individual or family or, better yet, for a complete line. In this way, you have the many family relationships readily viewable. Each family and individual are then lower level "tasks." The software allows you to expand or contract the time scale with a click of the mouse. You may also select, view and print specific task levels, allowing you to work with one individual or a single family group. This is all done with the underlying data unchanged. Reports can be generated of completed or incomplete research tasks. Since each task or milestone can have multiple "resources" assigned, one could get more sophisticated and use this as a reference to sources of the information.

I happened to have MS Project available from my profession. I realize that many people may not have this software at home, but there are some relatively inexpensive packages available.

—*Bill Hewitt*

Adding Historic Events to Timelines

I just read your article on timelines in the 23 September Ancestry Newsletter. In addition to preparing family timelines, I find it interesting—for myself and other family members who are less into the details—to include historical dates on my timeline. It shows what else was happening in the world.

For example, my great grandparents were married on 19 April 1865, just four days after President Lincoln was assassinated. I have also included historical and famous sports events. I include when each president was elected and the population of the U.S. at each census.

—John Vomhof

RootsWeb Town/County Database

When I am entering a lot of new information into my family tree software, I also keep the RootsWeb U.S. Town/County database <http://resources.rootsweb.com/cgi-bin/townco.cgi> open so that I can quickly use it to request a county and make my location entries complete the first time. It sure comes in handy for knowing counties for continued research.

— *Mary Ann (Smallwood) Bolton*
Mililani, HI

Update Your E-mail Address on Websites

I have questions, and I have some answers. But the e-mails I try to send keeps bouncing. Have you recently changed your e-mail address? It's time to go back to all those places you have posted queries and update your address. Now would be a good time to start a log of where you posted queries so that the next time you change your ISP you know where you need to go. Who knows what you are missing because no one can find you.

—*Diana R. Nelson*

Time Capsule Website

I am sending this tip as a follow-up regarding timelines. Read "dMarie Time Capsule" at <http://www.dmarie.com/timecap/>. You can type in a birth date and read top news headlines for that week; top songs; prices for bread, milk, eggs, car, house, stamps; the U.S. President and Vice President, and so on.

I look forward to the Quick Tips daily as well as on Tuesdays; I have them printed out as I do the *Ancestry Daily News*. I would love to see you do the Happy Dance. Thanks for all you and your staff do. You are a great lady.

— *Gladys*
Southern California

Thanks Gladys! You're a brave lady. The "happy dance" is not for the faint of heart.

— *Juliana*

Finding Images Online

A great resource for some remote viewing of your ancestor's neighborhood is the Google.com Search Engine. On its main page, you now have an option to click on one of four main categories. One of these categories, Images, gives you an opportunity to call up, say, all Internet images of Trenton, NJ, or Duluth, MN, or wherever your ancestor's home is. Not all are of genealogical interest, but many parks and scenic views will appear with the other clutter.

—Ray Marshall
Minneapolis

Great tip! A few weeks ago, I was looking for some information on my great-grandfather and decided to look for his hometown in Wyszkow, Poland. I found a little site called, Wyszkow.net. Although it was all in Polish, I decided to browse around and see if there were any pictures. Sure enough, under "Galeria" there was a whole section of photos, some of them historic. There is another section labeled "Historia," which I am hoping to get translated, as well as some maps with street names. It's so exciting to see your ancestor's hometown from halfway around the world!

—Juliana

Tracking Ancestors with GPS

I am active with the U.S. Coast Guard Aux and often use the Global Positioning System on water patrols. I am going to use GPS to search for my Revolutionary War ancestor. I can learn exactly where he was at given times of his life. This system can give his location within 35 feet. I already know where he was at Valley Forge, the church where he was married and many other events during his life, as well as his gravestone location.

A hand-held GPS can be purchased for this purpose for under $200. It can open up a whole new avenue for genealogists.

—Ron Ouimette

PDAs for Research and Travel

I was reading Beau Sharbrough's articles on using PDAs for research and I thought I'd share this with you.

Last year we traveled to England. I kept my full itinerary, contacts, and phone numbers on my PDA. I also used it to record all the information that I found on tombstones. I took pictures of the tombstones and as a backup (in case I cut something off in the pictures) I recorded the information on the stones onto my PDA. When I returned home I had everything written down. We also stopped into a historical society's office and I used my PDA to record all the information I could find in their books. The people at the society were amazed to see me writing everything down on my Palm instead of using pages and pages of paper. Of course, this was much easier to transport home as well as the PDA takes up very little space. Once home, I downloaded all of my newfound information to my computer. This is one of the handiest little gadgets around.

—Jeff Turl

Note: Beau's articles on PDAs can be found at:
Part I, Hardware
<http://www.ancestry.com/rd/prodredir.asp?sourceid=831&key=A506001>
Part II, Software
<http://www.ancestry.com/rd/prodredir.asp?sourceid=831&key=A516601>
Part III, Genealogy Software
<http://www.ancestry.com/rd/prodredir.asp?sourceid=831&key=A529301>
Part IV, The Kitchen Sink
<http://www.ancestry.com/rd/prodredir.asp?sourceid=831&key=A553401>

Keyboard Shortcuts Save Search Time

The other day, I was looking for a particular street in the 1930 Census for the District of Columbia. Namely, I was looking for North Capitol Street NW. Rather than reading through all the descriptions of the various districts, I typed on the "Ctrl" and "F" keys, to bring up a pop up of a box asking "Find What?" I typed in "Capitol," which gives you a broader search area since you do not know how E Capitol or East Capitol, N Capitol vs. North Capitol has been typed into the description. This saves on a great deal of time.

—Donna Mullen
St. Petersburg, Florida

Software Helps Decipher Poor Copies

I had a badly faded copy of a negative print of my daughter's birth certificate, which I was unable to make readable photocopies from. I scanned it into my Adobe Photoshop program and was able to adjust the contrast and lightness/darkness so that it was readable on the computer screen. Then when I printed it, the white on black showed up well so that I was able to read it again. This has also worked with difficult-to-read, pencil-written letters that have faded through the years.

—*Ruth Tucker*
Cedar Falls, Iowa

Store Your Notes on TreePad.com

Do you know TreePad? <www.treepad.com> It's ideal for keeping notes and texts subdivided however you like (in what they call "nodes," which anyone else would call file folders). It's easy to structure. The free version is useful, while the paid one also allows formatting and hyperlinks. However, it is not particularly good for graph-ics. (I have no association with the product, other than that I "couldn't live without it.")

— *Beth MacDonald*

Free Genealogy Software for Palms

I've finally found a great genealogy software for Palm Pilots and their kin—and it's free.

It's part of the Personal Ancestry File (PAF) software from the genealogy site provided by The Church of Jesus Christ of Latter-day Saints, Familysearch.org. With the tiny little Palm program you can carry around an amazingly complete set of family history information on your handheld computer. You can even send specific family information to a MemoPad file. It's very slick.

And best of all, if you're willing to take a few simple steps, you don't need to switch from your main genealogy program to use it. You simply tell your regular genealogy software to export a GEDCOM file, import that file into PAF, then choose File/Export and click on the Palm export radio button. Next time you synchronize the Palm Pilot with your desktop computer, it will grab the file and the Palm software.

If you don't want to navigate through the FamilySearch.org site, you can start with this page: <www.ldscatalog.com/cgi-bin/ncommerce3/CategoryDisplay?cgmenbr=1402&cgrfnbr=1678&RowStart=1&LocCode=FH>. Or you can go to the main page <www.familysearch.org page>, click on the Software tab at the top of the homepage and follow the links.

—*Richard A. Danca*
Newton, Massachusetts

Record Keeping Software

I use The Master Genealogist <www.whollygenes. com> for my primary record keeping. When I come across Witnesses, Executors, Partners, etc., that are not family members, I do enter them into my database as non-related (sometimes they turn out to be and I can then change the relationship without having to enter information a second time); then list them on the Witness Tag. In TMG, there is usually a place for principal and for witness(es) so that the record can be recalled with all attached names. I find this better than a separate list (as in a word processing document) because it can never be separated or misplaced from the original person's information.

It can also be done this way in several other programs that I play around with.

> —*Kim Paterson*
> *Heather & Thistle Genealogical Research*
> *Philadelphia Research*

"Died After" Dates

I have a lot of people in my family trees for whom I have no death date or place. In order to make it easier to keep in mind where and/or when I've found them alive (in a census, or an obituary's list of survivors, for instance), I record the information in my software's spot for recording deaths. I record it as Died: After [the date]. For the place, I type in "last found [the place]" if my source indicates such. Doing this helps in two ways.

1. It makes it much clearer where I might begin to look for more records when I have the opportunity.
2. When I upload the latest update of my file at Ancestry.com or RootsWeb.com, other researchers can get a better idea of whether the people in my files are of interest to them. My Benjamin Franklin and A. Lincoln Huffman, whom I last found alive in the 1880 census in Kansas, are not likely to be the same as someone in their family who shares the same name but who appears in the 1880 census in Ohio or who died in 1860.

—Susan Hopkins
Urbana, Illinois

Tips for Mac Users

I've noticed on some other genealogy websites that many of the data CD-ROMs are not available for those who happen to own a MAC computer. There is a software solution to this problem that should be helpful to those who may not know about it.

If you have a decently sized public library in your home area, go there and look for the *Macworld Mac Secrets*, 5th edition, by David Pogue & Joseph Schorr, copyrighted 1999. On the CD-ROM that comes with the book (a library 2nd checkout item), there are several programs that will help convert PC to Mac Files and back again, plus ways to convert, say, Word Perfect files into Claris Works files, so that you can access the data on the MAC. These are some of the programs available for MAC OS 7.5 & 8.0 systems-- and I would imagine can be used (or are updated versions for the latest OS 10) in the latest MAC versions. Chapter 16 in Mac Secrets, 5th edition, explains it all. I trust some MAC owners will find this information useful.

—Mike

Using MyFamily.com Sites

Using the MyFamily.com site, our family is focusing on each individual as their birthday comes up in 2002. We are asking for special memories about this person, funny things they have done or said, activities they've participated in, etc. This brings back some of the members who do not contribute regularly to the site.

For family members that many have never, and may never, meet, we are interviewing family members by phone and writing short summaries of their interests, activities, and plans for the future. This may draw more of them into the Web. Their pictures are featured on the cover photo and the scrolling announcement is about the featured cousin.

—Judy Utley Lyne

The Gift of Family History

I give all newlyweds a copy of my relatives' family history as I know it on the date of their wedding. They seem to be kept as family heirlooms.

I also give all newborns a personal genealogy with all their ancestors, documents about them, requisite charts and whatever photos I have.

As genealogists, we have priceless information that we have gathered and our families have shared with us. We have an obligation to pass it on. My philosophy is, it is never too early to publish, and I have been self-publishing my own and my wife's families' history for the past six years.

—*Leonard S. Duboff*
Bala Cynwyd, Pennsylvania

Old-Fashioned Home Improvement

I spent the last two days helping my eighty-six year-old father lever up a cement sidewalk, remove tree roots from under it, and put the sidewalk back together. Power tools failed, so we had to resort to shovels, wood blocks, hatchets, axes, saws, and human muscle power.

To me this was a very clear lesson in how hard our ancestors had to work to clear their land. When you multiply the work by an entire farm and for westward moves, it just becomes an astronomical amount of work. I wouldn't advise letting young children handle sharp tools, but doing a family project like this is a good way to teach them what clearing the land involved before the days of horses, mules, dynamite, power tools, and John Deere.

—*Kathy Kalin*

Remember Family with Photo Calendars

For Christmas this last year, I made a calendar for each of our kids and older grandkids. Everyone's birthdays and wedding anniversaries were noted on the calendars. The birthdays had a balloon bouquet there, and the anniversaries had a heart. On the page above, I put a picture of each of the birthday people for that month, taken when they were either a baby or very young. The pictures weren't put in any order, but each was numbered and matched a sheet that described each number. The family all seemed to really enjoy the calendars and had fun guessing who each person was. Along with this, they all now have pictures that they didn't have before. Some of these baby pictures were hard to come by and should be cherished. I enjoy reading all the tips each week!

—*Darlene Pinegar*

Photographs at Funerals

A member told us how she collected memories individually from friends and relatives at the time of a funeral, as many were too shy to speak.

When I lost a son several years ago some friends and relatives went through their pictures and loaned them to me so copies could be made. Some of these I had not seen and did not have. I recently lost a close friend and went through my own pictures so I could have copies made for her adult children. They were very pleased and said they would cherish them. These are pictures they probably would not have seen otherwise. I was pleased to be able to give them something of their mother's youth.

—Amy

Charm Bracelets Can Tell a Story

With the popularity of charm bracelets again in full swing, I got out my old ones from high school and turned them into a "Grandmother Bracelet." I ordered engravable charms and had one side lettered with the name of each grandmother on my mother's side, and the other side engraved with the year of birth. The dates go back to the 1600s. Everyone loves the bracelet!

What a gift such a bracelet would make for a teenage girl. After all, they are our "genealogists-in-training."

—Linda Fox

Keep Your Family Tree Creative

I ran off a copy of a descendant chart and use it to keep my files in order. As I get an obituary, wedding invitation, newspaper article, marriage license, birth certificate, etc., I file it in the descendant chart in order of the appropriate person's name. When I show it to relatives, they not only see what I have done but also what kind of source information I'm looking for. Wedding invitations and funeral programs get the biggest response. Some want copies and some volunteer copies of the ones they have. These items, along with photos, make the tree less dry and encourage family to get involved.

—*Allan Nugent*

Collaborative Family Recipe Book

Two years ago, I asked each family member to submit three of their favorite recipes and tell me why or when they served that particular dish, or any other anecdote that went with the dish. Everyone (including the children) sent in recipes, and I made a family cookbook.

I also included photos that I had taken over the previous year, most of them at our annual family golf tournament. I laminated the cover and back of the book as well as the divider pages. Then I spiral-bound the whole works and tied a bookmark with tassel on the bottom to one of the spirals. I gave them to each family unit as a Christmas gift. Everyone seemed very pleased with their family cookbook—with some family "history" thrown in as well!

—*Jeff Turl*

Family History Skit

My cousin took our family history and made a skit out of it. To keep the children interested, she put hats in a bag and made a cardboard sign that said who the hat belonged to. People were then asked to take a bag and act out whoever's name was in the bag. This was a great hit as the skit got everyone interested in the family history.

—*Kathleen Honce*

Family Calendar for Memories

If you haven't already begun to keep a yearly family calendar, maybe you'll want to do so. I have kept mine since 1967. These calendars remind me of the chronological order of what I did and when I did it. My collection of calendars shows a move, baby appointments, little league games, even a driving test. I wish one of my ancestors had done something like this. I use a journal to expound on these events if I want to.

But right now my calendars remind me of a lot of fun events.

—*Sharon More*

Family Tree Heirloom Quilt

I printed out old ancestors' pictures I had scanned into my computer onto t-shirt transfer paper, then transferred them to squares of material. I then made a quilt with the squares, and used brown, heavy thread to embroider a tree to connect them in order. I gave one to my sister's oldest son and his wife, and one to my oldest son and his wife. If they are cared for properly, they will go down the line for many generations and hopefully awaken a few genealogists in my descendants!

—*Lori Jett*

E-Mailing List for Extended Family

My family has extended family members that most of us have never met. My husband's family is spread from various locations in Ireland and other countries, and all over the United States.

A cousin in Ireland came up with a wonderful idea. Many of us have access to e-mail now. He e-mailed about ten people and asked each to introduce themselves to the others. People responded to him and he e-mailed the responses he received to the group. They sent this to other family members and the list grew. Personal introduction is purely voluntary. We were surprised at how many people responded.

Each introduction was placed with the appropriate person in the Family Tree. Currently, people who haven't seen each other in years are corresponding. The cousin in Ireland has been sending "The Way It Was" stories about growing up in Ireland (fascinating!). What a treasure to personally get to know those living relatives. I believe the list is up to twenty-six people now.

—*Kate Vaughan*

Ancestry.com hosts free U.S. and European White Pages at: <www.ancestry.com/rd/redir.asp?sourceid=831&targetid=3485>

—*eds.*

Middle Initials, Last Names

We all know that indexes are helpful, but we also know that the wonderful folks who created them don't know how you spell the surname you're looking for. So I have lists of variations in spellings that I use whenever I search an index. I've created these lists over the years, while researching. Most of the lists are possible variations on the way the name might be misspelled depending on pronunciation in various parts of the country. Other variations are dependent on an understanding of old handwriting, like how "f" could be "s" and "u," and how "v" or "n" sometimes get interchanged.

Today, I stumbled across something entirely new. I was searching for a family I know was in Weakley Co., TN, in 1840, but the name was not in the index on Ancestry. On the images online index, I entered the date, state, and county and was going page by page looking for possible variations on the name. Suddenly, something else showed up, a Francis A. Kemp.

I've researched him for years and know all about him in 1840, but the name in the index showed up as Francis Akemp, in the index under "A" not "K." I went to the page on the census and sure enough, the end of the "A" flows right into the "K," which does look lower case. Now I have another index idea, look for the middle initial just in case it became attached to the surname.

—Leslie Bell

Voice Recognition Software

Faced with the task of transcribing a number of old hand-written letters so that they could be annotated and easily made available to others, I purchased voice recognition software (Via Voice, $70) and read the letters into my word processor. The software "trains" itself to understand your voice. After the first few letters were read, the error rate decreased significantly, taking much of the drudgery out of the whole typing process.

—*Barry McGhan*
Ann Arbor, Michigan

New Anglo Italian Mailing List

I set up the Anglo Italian Mailing list, which is hosted by RootsWeb.com, in January 2002. This was to be a discussion forum for those of us in the UK researching our Italian ancestry, but it became apparent, very early on, that a more formal society was needed. Through the mailing list, a small group of us gathered "virtually" together and set about organizing a formal Anglo Italian Family History Society. We had an Inaugural meeting at the venue for the Society of Genealogist Fair, here in the UK on 4 May 2002, which was well attended. The Anglo Italian Family History Society was then formally launched. We welcome and encourage new members. We are currently organizing and planning various transcription projects to aid fellow Anglo Italian Researchers.

A membership form is available for downloading via:

<http://www.dreamwater.net/anglersrest/aifhsform.htm>

The Society webpage is still under construction, but the mailing list page is available via:

<http://www.dreamwater.net/anglersrest/Italian.htm>

For any further information please send e-mail to the address at the bottom of this page. ("Anglers Rest")

—Julie Goucher

Learn about Indiana Research

The Necrology file for Saint Joseph County, Indiana, U.S. now encompasses obituaries from 1 January 1920 through 31 December 1989 for any current or former residents of the county.

This is a current indexing project of the Saint Joseph County Public Library in South Bend, Indiana, that volunteers are inputting into a computer for subsequent availability on the Internet. The 1990s are the current decade being worked on. This file is searchable with either complete or incomplete names but not browseable. There are nearly 25,000 entries for the 1980s database.

Go to <http://www.sjcpl.lib.in.us/necrology/necrology.html>, select from which decade/database that the search is desired, enter as much of the name as is known, and click on SEARCH.

Thank you for your help in letting others know of this resource for family historians.

—*Stephen Elek, Jr.*
SJCPL Volunteer

Coroners' Reports

I recently came across an article on coroners' reports. It states that coroners' reports are available for public review and are usually located in the County Clerk's office. If the coroners' reports are not at the County Clerk's office desk, ask the local coroner where his archives are located and when the office is open to review the records. It's interesting what you can find in the records. I know that most of the records will be in medical terminology but the report will make an interesting addition to your family history archives. I have started a "medical" listing in my family papers to see what all the relatives have passed away from. It will also give you an idea of what diseases or problems may run in the family.

—*Kaye Jonas*

Create a Precautionary Health History

I was curious about my great-grandfather's early death in 1869 in Iowa. (He was in his thirties.) When I found no local record, someone suggested that I check the 1870 mortality schedule. Since he died in October 1869, I stupidly rejected the idea that he could be on that list. When I finally researched the list, I did locate him and found that reason given for death was bowel cancer. What a find. That line of my family has a sad history of stomach and bowel cancer. When I told the doctor at the Mayo Clinic about my find, the doctor requested I prepare a family tree of the stomach or bowel cancer in that line of my family. With this information, they now watch and test very regularly. Although they perform more extensively and more frequently than they normally would, I have had no problems with my insurance company paying. Even the younger doctors have been quite interested in this family health tree, which has been in my record for quite a few years now. Incidentally, I have been very lucky so far, possibly due to early polyp removal, watching diet, etc.—all because I found this information.

—*Wanda Spainhower*

Check Highway Markers for Clues

The next time you drive down the highway, be sure to consider those neatly painted cast-iron Highway Markers. They contain a nugget of valuable history, and you may even find, if you are in the neighborhood of a family ancestor, a bit of genealogy related to your own family.

On the other hand, feel free to ask individuals of an area known to have strong ties to your family if they have seen such a sign that may indicate the name of your ancestor.

Is this an unrealistic suggestion? Not at all. Consider my own example . . .

Franklin Ayres Comly was "thirty years president of the North Pennsylvania railroad" and chose to name a station in 1876 after his mother, contracting her name, Elizabeth Ayres, into "Bethayres." This act is memorialized in a highway marker, to be seen to this day.

Highway markers are full of valuable material, but are, sadly, disappearing as thieves and vandals take their toll. Why not keep an eye of interest on these fascinating gems of history?

—*Vince Summers*

Homebound Family History Tips

http://www.ancestry.com/rd/prodredir.asp?sourceid=831&key=A585906

I just read George Morgan's article about making the most of your research time while at home and look forward to incorporating these ideas during times when I'm homebound. Currently, when I cannot get out to do research, I spend time doing several things:

1. Review my family tree database and various records (census, vital statistics, obituaries, etc.). I may find clues—or errors!—that I missed before.
2. Record sources in the database, and on copies of records, using correct documentation methods. I often find my previous documentation needs tweaking to be in a correct format.
3. Read up on my ancestors' culture and locations in their time period, whether the sources be online, books, or magazines. Perhaps a phone call to my great-aunt would reveal bits of my ancestors' social history.
4. Label photographs.
5. Clean up my file system. (Yuck!)
6. Play with my kids. Have fun and create some memories with them. Who knows? Perhaps stories about these memories will be passed on to my great-great-great grandkids!

— Jenny Davis

Travel Tip

Last summer, I traveled from Chicago to New York City, and had the opportunity to meet some "long lost cousins" we hadn't seen since we were about seven or eight years old. We were also hoping to go into "the city" to visit the church where my grandfather was baptized, and where he and my grandmother were married. I have a looseleaf binder filled with information I have gathered on many of my ancestors. I tucked this into my suitcase, amazed at how much room it took, but more amazed at how much it weighed.

As I traveled around the city, I carried my precious book and groaned about the weight and inconvenience. Finally, while in a store, I had an idea.

I purchased a simple address book and copied the names, date of birth, marriage, spouse, death date and death place for each person. That way, I had easy access to the basic information and could easily answer questions.

In no way does it replace the information I have in my binder, but since then, I have frequently carried the book in my purse so I could do a quick lookup when necessary. I enter the new information I find and then transfer it into the binder when I have time.

—*Eileen Tierney*

Conference Daily Planner

As I planned and packed to attend a conference, I made up a chart (I use a table with columns for Tuesday through Sunday) for each hour of each day during the conference week. I listed luncheons and the banquet, in their time slots. I also listed the lecture that I most wanted to attend for each hour I had open. For talks I might not attend but would like to purchase an audiotape of, I wrote in a big red "T." I still do check out the syllabus and on-site program to be sure I have made the best choice for my research needs or may add a session that just looks interesting. I add the actual rooms for each meal and lecture to my chart once I am at the conference. During the week, I highlight the sessions and meals that are completed. This makes it easier to zoom in on where I need to go next.

—*Paula Stuart Warren*
St. Paul, Minnesota

Wife Listed under Husband's Name?

Only fifty or sixty years ago, some small town newspapers had a Society editor. I recall telling my wife when I read the obituary of Mrs. James Doe, that this lady couldn't even die with her own name, "Mary Doe." Be careful when searching for ancestors that you don't overlook the loss of an individual to the rules of those social editors.

—*S.J. Feit*

Navy Ships Online

If anyone is looking for information on Navy ships, such as ship history, photographs, etc., a good site is <www.lonesailor.org>. This site is for the Navy Heritage Center in Washington, D.C., which is the home of the Navy Memorial and the Lone Sailor sculpture.

—Walter J. Bank

Find Clues in Medical Records

I have been looking for a particular great-grandfather for a year, and finally found a clue by writing for his medical records that pertain to genealogical questions, not medical history. Hospitals and nursing homes will, with the proper signed release, provide medical records on your old lost relatives. At least, they did in my search.

—Richard Scott

Township Atlas of the United States

The tip from Pat Herrick reminded me of how many times I have seen a query asking for the location of a town in Arkansas where their ancestor was enumerated for the census, when researchers aren't able to find the town on a map. I go to Township Atlas of The United States, 1990, 1991, Andriot Documents Index, a large book found in the reference section of our county library.

Alabama has divisions, Arkansas townships, Mississippi districts, Louisiana police jury wards, and the list goes on. Each state is different. In Arkansas, where townships are used, there will often be a town with the same name of the township, the town shown in uppercase letters. I have found this book to be a valuable aid.

—*Ellen Hernandez*

Request a Better Copy

I've received several death certificates that were difficult to read, and I've sent them back to the Vital Records Department of the state involved and asked for a better copy. In every case I've received a much better copy the second time. I did it with the Social Security Administration with some SS-5 forms and received remarkably better and more legible copies. We're paying good money; we might as well receive good copies.

—Bill Davis
Atlanta, Georgia

JewishGen Helps with Emigration Research

I put your column on "Building a Locality File" away to read when I got time, which I just did. I think the JewishGen site <www.shtetlinks.jewishgen.org> has taken it one step further. Many of us (or our parents or grandparents) have emigrated from places that do not exist anymore, and therefore we are trying to build sites for those places. The site will contain documents that are translated from their original language, information from books, stories and pictures. I am coordinating three of these.

It isn't easy to do for places where the Jewish population has not existed for over fifty years, and those who immigrated seventy to one hundred years ago went to North America, South America, Palestine and possibly other places scattered around the world. We see it as a way of leaving a legacy for those who follow us and want to find out something about where their families lived.

On the site about Litin, I have prepared a time-chart. I have integrated the facts and figures I know about Litin together with the history of Europe and Jewish history to give a comprehensive view of what may have influenced various aspects of life in this city. I plan on creating a similar chart for each of the other two sites.

— Rose Feldman

Swedish Emigrants

I'm a Swede, and I manage a data bank for Swedish emigrants from Sweden to America. I do that for the Skanes Genealogiska Forbund, SGF, and indirectly for the Svenska Emigrantinstitutet in Vaxjo, EMI. the data bank contains over one million emigrants from Sweden who went abroad during the years 1845-1950. I am working with the emigrants from the Swedish province of Scania and our portion of the data bank contains about 170,000 people. You can find us online at <http://www.sgf.m.se> and <http://www.swemi.nu>. Don't hesitate to contact us!

—*Ake Kjellqvist*

American WWII Orphans Network

American World War II Orphans Network (AWON) has a website at <www.awon.org> with a lot of information on how to find WWII military records, buddies, units, unit reunions, etc. Non-members can tap into that information at the website. There is also a book, *Touchstones*, written by AWON founder Ann Mix, available through the AWON bookstore, at the site.

Any family member of a military person killed in WWII is eligible to join AWON and participate in even more information.

—*Alece Egan*

Visit Senior Centers

During a recent reunion, we began discussing the various sources of information one could use to learn about deceased family members. One aunt brought up a tip that I had not heard of before: Go to senior citizen centers and rest homes in the areas where you are looking for information. For example, my great-grandfather was from the cities of Licking and Success in Texas County, Missouri. I could then get a list of the various centers and rest homes in those cities, to find citizens who knew or had heard of my great-grandfather.

— Wally Caviness
Bellingham, Washington

Surname Buddy and Mailing Lists

I have surname listings on my buddy list as well as a mailing list for each family name in my e-mail address book that includes everyone I e-mail information to for that surname.

The names are automatically sorted in order, and I don't have to type in contact information every time I find something they might be interested in. I just pop up the named e-mail mailing list for that series of names.

Occasionally, I will send out an update to everyone to make sure I am covered on all names and all information has been updated from my end of the Internet line. Thank you.

—*Jane Bart*
Las Vegas, Nevada

Keep a File of Unrelated Folks

I keep track of all the "other folks" in a family file database titled "Strangers in the Night." Some may be related by blood (but I haven't proven it); others may have been listed as a witness of a birth in pension papers, attended the same birthday party according to a local newspaper, or just had the same name and lived in the same area. Those other folks pop up everywhere! When a name sounds familiar, I open my "Strangers in the Night" file. I've found several relatives by keeping a file of strangers.

—*Denise Gesner*

Interview Family Friends

Unfortunately for me, my interest in ancestry came after my father was gone and my mother was too ill to question. However, a friend of hers since grade school and another friend of the family since she was in her twenties have been full of information, as is my dad's sister.

To obtain new information, I simply scheduled a date with them and brought over my parents' old photo albums so they could review the pictures. As they tell me things, I jot notes on post-its and stick them on the page with the photo. I've also taken my video camera and let it run while they look at the photos. It's wonderful the information they are providing that I am unable to get from my parents. So, don't forget your parents' friends. I'm sure they'd love to hear from you and reminisce.

— *Laura Nichols*

Memories from Another Generation

My mother-in-law was visiting so I had her help me find family in the 1930 U.S. Census on Ancestry.com. Where I had not lived in this town for over thirty years, she was a wealth of information on exactly where streets were located. As a result I was quickly able to pinpoint the areas I need to look for family. She was thrilled when we found her and her parents in the census.

I was especially fond of the stories she told as I read off names of neighbors or old school friends. I also found relatives that I didn't know about. She would say things like "oh that person was my cousin on my father's mother side." So if you have an older relative coming to visit, you might want to have them sit next to you when you are reading a census. You will find out a lot about what they did growing up in the 1930s.

— Linda Rosedahl

Form a Research Partnership

Forming research partnerships with others can be very productive. My husband's grandmother emigrated from Friesland, Netherlands. I was able to form a partnership with a researcher living in the same area of the Netherlands. We included a researcher who had resided in the same area as she, but who now lives in the United States. The Netherlands researcher did much research for me in the local Friesland archives, and the United States researcher found marriages and obits for us. In exchange, I researched some branches of their families at the Family History Library. This partnership not only sped up research, but helped with the language barriers we face when researching in an unfamiliar language and or locale.

—*Ened Roughton*

Soliciting Information

When contacting other researchers, don't ask for information about living people. You're much more likely to ensure cooperation if you make it clear that you're only interested in deceased ancestors. I've had two people ask for information about my family (children, grandchildren, etc.) which I'm thankful I didn't provide; I found that one of them had posted the information I did give her on the Internet.

It's also wise when you're sending information to eliminate details concerning living people. My cutoff point is at my grandparents who are deceased now.

—*Joyce Clark*

Heirloom Photo Ornaments

A few years ago, my husband's grandmother gave us more than 100 of the photos from her collection because she thought it would be nice to "give you faces to go with all those names." What a wonderful gift! I promptly scanned them and burned a CD, intending to share the CD with my husband's siblings.

Then, last year, my husband's father gave us a trunk that sat at the end of his bed "getting in the way for years." It contained a gold mine of genealogy information that his grandmother had researched on the family, as well as hundreds of photographs—several of them tintypes! We were overwhelmed with gratitude and again promptly scanned the photographs and papers and burned a CD with the intent to share copies of it.

There was only minimal interest in "family tree stuff" from my husband's siblings. However, they were incredibly interested in the people in the pictures. Last year, our Christmas tree was a memory tree. I bought small photo frames a little at a time over the year, and by the end of the year we had enough to represent each family member that we had photographs for, at least once. I printed the pictures with name and pertinent dates at the bottom.

This year, copies of what I have done for our tree will be gifts for my husband's siblings. I am making a small card for each one and attaching each picture to it with a small bio of the subject and a little about the event photographed (where known). On the card will be a copy of the photo in the frame. I am also including a scrapbook that eventually all the photo cards can be placed in.

—*Dawn Kifer*

Pedigree Christmas Cards

I made a very simple Christmas card by folding a piece of red construction paper in half and then decorating the front with glitter. I then drew a very simple family tree, using two 8" x 11" pieces of white paper. I included only the grandmothers and grandfathers on my mother's side, going back ten generations. I am sending them to all my nieces and nephews. Next year, I hope to be able to do the same thing on my father's side.

—*Virginia Atkins Scott (née Buzzell)*

Create a Family Migration Map

For Christmas, one of our sons took a large map of the United States and traced the migrations of different branches of our family around the U.S. with various colored pens. You could also use colored string and fasten the map to a porous surface.

—*Maxine Johnson*

Shadow Boxes Display Heirlooms

I noticed at the craft store that in addition to a big surge in books and products to make family history scrapbooks, the store has a large selection of shadow boxes. I purchased several of them to make various displays.

I have my grandfather's calling card and several calling cards and valentines he saved in a picture frame. I put a crushed velour cloth over the back cardboard of the frame and also added a small picture of my grandfather. In addition, I put a bone-handled pocketknife, which he was always whittling with in another, smaller shadow box. My husband's picture, World War II medals and a citation from the president, received after my husband's death went together in yet another shadow box to display. My mother had a tiny little doll for which my grandmother crocheted a dress. I put this in its own shadow box frame. My great-grandmother had a pin, which is going to be put in yet another shadow box.

This is an excellent way to protect and display family heirlooms. Most craft stores offer classes or will help you design and complete your display. For years it has been difficult to find the shadow boxes but now there are many of them in different sizes, available for all our memorabilia.

—*Bette*

Remember to protect your valuables from direct sunlight, which can fade textiles, photos, and documents and cause irreparable damage. Copies of photos and documents can be used in place of those valuable originals and can be "antiqued" by staining them with tea.

—*eds.*

Family Reunion Icebreakers

During a family reunion, have a different colored ribbon pin for each branch of a family. When people see a branch of a different color they can ask look for a common ancestor and find out how the branches tie into each other. You could also have photos, a family group sheet, and/or pedigree chart with the corresponding ribbons to designate each branch as a reference point.

The ribbons are easy to make and inexpensive; you just need a bit of ribbon and a small safety pin.

Old photos on poster boards and storyboards are also great icebreakers. You can use inexpensive laser copies of old photos and baby photos and not risk damage or loss to your precious family photos. Arrange the poster board with photos and use the ribbon to signal which branch of the family the photos are from.

—*Gaila*

Websites for Quilting

If you are interested in creating a quilt that has family photographs on the fabric, Hewlett Packard has a website that tells you how to print directly onto fabric using freezer paper to bond to the fabric while it goes through the printer <www.homeandoffice.hp.com/hho/us/eng/ fabric_sheets.html>.

There is also a general page for quilters with lots of ideas and instructions at <http://h30039.www3.hp.com/>.

—Marie Brewer

Index

C

Cable modem, protecting from power surges, 85

Calendars, family, 117, 123

Cameras, digital, 74

Cards, business c. for genealogy conference attendees, 50

Cemeteries. *See also Tombstones*

Battle of the Bulge, 25

contacting those who visit a grave, 26

county map and, 57

documenting location, 17, 20

finding with Topozone.com, 73

living relatives and, 23

local genealogical societies and, 27

photographing landmarks, 18

photos, labeling, 19

precautions for visiting, 21

transfer of remains, 16

war cemeteries, requesting pictures of headstones, 25

Census indexes

printing census images on back of, 41

researching, 38

Census names, deciphering, 40

Census records, African-American, 37

Censuses

boarders in, 68

census takers, 42

checkoff sheet, 45

first/last name reversed, 43

reviewing with relatives, 147

Charm bracelets, 119

Checkoff sheet for censuses, 45

Childrens' art/schoolwork, saving, 5

Christmas migration maps, 153

Christmas ornaments, photo, 151

Church records of cemeteries (local genealogical society), 27

Citing sources, 64

Colored paper, using with microfilm, 59

Conferences, genealogy

business cards for, 50

tips, 135

Contacting those who visit family grave sites, 26

Contacts, tracking genealogy, 70

Cookies, springerlie rolling pin, 2

Copies

helping ensure legible, 67

keeping track of source, 64

Coroners' reports, 130

County map and cemeteries, 57

Precautions
  when giving out information, 150
  when visiting cemeteries, 21
Precinct or town?, 32
Printing on photo paper, 58
Project management software, creating timelines with, 99
Protecting
  genealogical information, 84-89
  oversize documents, 91

Q
Queries, keep email address updated in, 102
Quilt, family tree, 124
Quilting web sites, 156

R
Random acts of Genealogical kindness, 47
Rechecking databases, 98
Recipe book, family, 121
Recording gravesites' locations, 17
Relatives
  living r. and cemeteries, 23
  reviewing census with, 147
Remains, transfer of, 16
Research

performing from home, 133
  using PDAs for, 106, 110
Research partnerships, 149. *See also Buddy list*
Rest homes, 144
Restoration, photo r. website, 75
Reunions, icebreakers for, 155
Reversing names, 43
Rings, wedding (story), 1
Rolling pin, springerle, 2
Rolodex for genealogy, 66
RootsWeb US Town/County database, 101

S
Safeguarding. *See Protecting*
Safety tips for visiting cemeteries, 21
Scanning faded documents, 108
School work, saving children's, 5
Scrapbooks, 80, 81, 83
Search tip for saving time, 107
Senior Centers, 144
Shadow boxes, 154
Sharing information, 46-48
Ships
  domestic travel lists, 8
  naval, 137

About the Author

Juliana S. Smith has been the editor of the *Ancestry Daily News* and *Ancestry Weekly Digest* since 1998. Together, the newsletters reach over 1.25 million subscribers via e-mail. She is also the author of *The Ancestry Family Historian's Address Book* and has written for *Ancestry* Magazine and *Genealogical Computing*. Juliana works from her home in Indiana where she lives with her husband, six-year-old daughter, two dogs, and two cats. In her spare time, she enjoys chasing down her own ancestors.